the Greenville Reformed
Church - 1842

the Arms of the Reformed
Church in America

Nisi Dominus Frustra

Eendracht maakt Macht

ty Bell of
n the Church
Ave. at 48 st

The Reformed Church
at Bronxville, N.Y.
1926

Pulpit in the old
Church

the Reformed Church
at Bronxville, N.Y.
Built - 1850

"O SEND OUT THY LIGHT AND THY TRUTH"

A HISTORY OF
THE REFORMED CHURCH
OF BRONXVILLE
NEW YORK

A HISTORY OF THE
Reformed Church
of Bronxville

IN COMMEMORATION OF ITS CENTENARY

NOVEMBER 5, 1950

———————◆———————

Edited by Mrs. Harry Leslie Walker
and LaMont A. Warner

End-Papers and Pen Sketches
by LaMont A. Warner

———————◆———————

PUBLISHED BY

THE CONSISTORY OF THE CHURCH

BRONXVILLE, NEW YORK

1951

DEDICATED

TO

THE MEN, WOMEN AND CHILDREN

OF THIS CHURCH

WHO,

GUIDED BY HIS SPIRIT,

HAVE LABORED FOR THE GROWTH OF

THE KINGDOM OF GOD

FOREWORD

———◆———

ᴴERE is the story of a Church, compiled as the milestone of a hundred years is passed. Let it call forth
a just homage to the goodly heritage that is herein
recorded.

This book is issued at a time when the congregation
of the Reformed Church of Bronxville is united, responsive and moving forward with thrilling strides. It is a
fitting time indeed to thank God for the past, to take
heart in the present, and to face our tomorrow with
confidence. I believe this volume will play its part on
each score.

To the several hands and hearts whose labors have
brought this account to its present form, heartfelt
appreciation is warmly accorded.

The words of Paul may well serve as both foreword
and conclusion: "Seeing we also are compassed about
with so great a cloud of witnesses, let us lay aside every
weight, and the sin which doth so easily beset us, and
let us run with patience the race that is set before us,
looking unto Jesus the author and finisher of our faith."

LOWELL RUSSELL DITZEN

CONTENTS

LIST OF ILLUSTRATIONS

DRAWINGS IN THE TEXT

THE PHOTOGRAPHS

PREFACE

EARLY in 1950, the Consistory of the Reformed Church of Bronxville, New York, resolved to publish a history of the church to commemorate its first hundred years. A Church History Committee was appointed, composed of the following: John L. Carson, chairman; William J. Cunningham, O. Dickinson Street and Mrs. Harry Leslie Walker, with Thomas B. Gilchrist, ex-officio, as president pro tem of Consistory.

Bertrand G. Burtnett, the Village Historian, was asked to collect historical data pertaining to the subject. Through access to the church files, and to early as well as current issues of the local newspapers, he was able to furnish much valuable material.

Important information with regard to certain chapters of the book was supplied to the History Committee as follows: on the Church School, by Mrs. Otto J. Gette; on the Women's Society, by Mrs. Franklin S. Whitehouse, archivist of the Society; on the Men's Club, by Thomas B. Gilchrist; on Music, by Jackson Kinsey; on World Wide Interests, by Mrs. A. L. Warnshuis; and on Memorials by Harry Leslie Walker. At the request of the committee, Dr. Ditzen has graciously written a chapter on The Future.

LaMont A. Warner, a former resident of Bronxville and officer of the church, and Assistant Professor of Fine Arts at Teachers College, Columbia University, was asked to edit the material and he kindly offered to furnish illustrations for the book.

Members of the History Committee rendered valuable assistance, as did Mrs. Revellese and Mrs. DuPuy of the church staff. Hubert A. Howson, clerk of Consistory, was tireless in clarifying obscure points and preparing data for lists in certain categories.

The final editing, preparation of the text for the press, and indexing were done by Mrs. Walker.

CHAPTER I

EARLY HISTORY OF THE REFORMED
CHURCH IN EUROPE AND AMERICA
1550 - 1850

THE Reformed Church in America had its inception in Europe during the sixteenth century, when there was a secession from the Roman Catholic Church by many great religious leaders. Among these were Martin Luther of Germany (1483-1546), Erasmus of Rotterdam (1467-1536), Wessel of Holland (1419-1489), John Calvin of Geneva (1509-1564) and Zwingli of Switzerland (1484-1531).

Charles V (1500-1558), King of Spain and Holy Roman Emperor, had inherited the Netherlands in 1506. He was an ardent Catholic and was determined to crush Protestantism throughout his empire. The result was that thousands of persons were massacred during his reign. In 1555 Charles V relinquished the Netherlands to his son Philip II, whose merciless general, the Duke

1

of Alva, ravaged the Netherlands in an attempt to suppress the Dutch revolt against the cruel tyranny of the Spanish rulers. However, in spite of persecution, the Reform movement spread, and countless religious martyrs went to the stake, singing hymns of praise in which multitudes joined.

In 1568, William of Nassau, Prince of Orange, came to the rescue of the persecuted people. The Spaniards were driven back in 1573. In 1579, deputies of various counties and duchies in the Low Countries met and agreed upon a Treaty of Union, which was published in the Town House of Utrecht. This document is regarded as the foundation of the Dutch Republic. It contains twenty-six articles defining the rights and powers of the component parts of the Union.

Two years later, in 1581, a declaration of independence from the domination of Spain was issued by the deputies of the united provinces assembled at The Hague.

The Constitution of the Dutch Republic became famous. Her scholars and universities, her diplomacy and tolerance were known throughout the continent. The Reformed Protestant doctrines, formulated at that time, were adopted by the Holland Church.

After another half-century of struggle, both political and religious, the Thirty Years' War was brought to an end in 1648 by the Peace of Westphalia. The independence of Switzerland and the Netherlands was established, and treaties were made between various conflicting nations. Of even greater significance than the territorial redistribution, were the ecclesiastical provisions of the Peace which guaranteed equal rights to Protestants and Catholics in continental Europe; and thus demonstrated the fact that Protestantism could no more be crushed than Roman Catholicism could be Protestantized.

Therefore, the year 1648 and the Peace of Westphalia mark one of the milestones in the progress of the history of religion.

When one considers the heroic leadership of William, Prince of Orange, and the fact that Holland gained her freedom through his wise guidance it is not surprising that when the officials of the Reformed Church in America desired an emblem which should be at once commemorative and representative, they appropriated the coat-of-arms of one who had fathered both the country and the church of their ancestors.

The emblem now in use in the Reformed Church in America is an adaptation of the coat-of-arms of William the Silent, Prince of Orange, and represents the principalities of which he was ruler or to which he was related. The first quarter of the large shield bears the arms of Nassau. It has a gold lion rampant, on a blue field surrounded by seventeen gold billets, representing the union of the ten States of the Netherlands with the seven States of Holland under William. The second quarter represents Katzenelnbogen and has a red lion rampant guardant, crowned, on a gold field. The third quarter represents Vianden, and has a red field banded with silver. The fourth quarter has two gold lions pas-

3

sant guardant, on a red field, and is the shield of Dietz.

The small shield is also quartered. The first and fourth quarters, bearing diagonal bands of gold on a red field, represent the principalities of Chalons; the second and third quarters, with a horn or bugle suspended on a gold field, that of Orange. These martial horns symbolize the courageous leadership of those who took up arms against the Moors and Saracens.

The smallest shield is that of Jane of Geneva, who married one of the princes of Orange. It is divided into nine squares, five of which have gold, and four blue fields.

The crown surmounting the helmet, which is the symbol of bravery in war, represents the Emperor

Charles V who granted the princes of Orange the right to place the imperial crown above the shield.

To adapt the coat-of-arms for use as a church emblem, the pillars and stars were added to direct men's thoughts upwards to the Life Eternal. The emblem is made complete by the addition of the Latin motto *Nisi Dominus Frustra,* "Without the Lord all is vain" placed above and the old Dutch watchword *Eendracht Maakt Macht,* "Union makes Strength" placed below.

While this period of political and religious struggle was taking place in Europe, the great colonizing movement to the newly discovered land across the Atlantic took on real significance.

In 1609, Henry Hudson, the English navigator, sailing under the auspices of the Dutch East India Company, discovered the river which bears his name. Soon a flourishing trade in valuable furs was established by ships plying between Europe and the "Great River from the Mountains" as the Hudson River was called.

Because of this important trade, a new organization known as the Dutch West India Company was chartered in 1621.

Two years later Holland established in America the province of New Netherland, and the following year thirty families were brought over by the Dutch West India Company in the ship New Netherland. Most of these families were Walloons, which was a name (meaning strangers) given by the Dutch to those inhabitants of southern Netherlands who spoke French instead of Flemish.

Upon arriving in America they settled for the most part on Governor's Island, Staten Island and at Wallabout (Walloons Bought or Cape), in and near New York Harbor; although some families continued the journey up the Hudson River to settle at Fort Orange (Albany).

Religious persecutions continuing in Europe, America now became a haven for the oppressed who came in large numbers: Huguenots from France, Protestants from the German Palatinate, Pilgrims from England and Covenanters from Scotland. Some of these colonists came by way of the Netherlands to New York and New Jersey. It was those from Holland who became the fathers of the Dutch Reformed Church in America.

Inasmuch as sailors of the company were often away from their homes for long periods of time, the charter of the Dutch East India Company had required that when colonists were sent out, chaplains should be provided to minister to the spiritual needs of the sailors on shipboard, and settlers should be provided with a Dominie at the expense of the company. By an oversight, these provisions had been omitted from the charter of the Dutch West India Company.

In 1624, the Consistory* of Amsterdam called the omission to the consideration of the Directors of the company who resolved that: "Attention to the religious services be paid both on ship board and on land." They then asked the Consistory to recommend a suitable "Comforter of the Sick." Bastiaen Jansen Kroll and Jan

* For explanation of terms *Consistory* and *Classis*, see Appendix.

6

Huyck were sent over with Peter Minuit and they "read to the commonality on Sunday, texts of Scripture and the creeds, and set the Psalms." In the absence of a minister they could conduct church services, reading Scripture and prayers and a sermon written by a regularly ordained minister.

New Netherland being now a province, as noted above, Peter Minuit, a Christian merchant and pioneer, was appointed Director General in 1626. When he arrived in Manhattan, he found it to be a fur-trading center of the Indians from whom he purchased the entire island, containing some twenty-two thousand acres of land, for trinkets valued at about sixty guilders or twenty-four dollars. He immediately began to build a suitable fort which at first was a simple blockhouse encircled by red cedar palisades backed with earthworks. This was called Fort Amsterdam and the growing town became known as New Amsterdam and was headquarters of the Dutch West India Company.

In the spring of 1628 when the colony numbered two hundred and seventy souls, the Rev. Jonas Michaelius came to New Amsterdam as the first minister of the colony. He was then forty-four years old, had been graduated from the University of Leyden and had served one of the "churches under the cross" in Brabant. He was pastor at Nieu Bokswonde in 1612, and at Hew in 1614, and had served as chaplain on the coast of New Guinea before coming to the little cluster of rude houses at the lower end of Manhattan Island. He proceeded at once to the organization of a church.

7

In the Reformed Church, organization is normally effected by a committee of a Classis within the bounds of the proposed new church. This committee meets with the people who desire to be organized into a church, receives the letters of church membership of such as may join by transfer from other churches, hears the confessions of faith of others, supervises the election of elders and deacons from among their number, and then declares the congregation constituted into a church.

Since there existed no Classis or committee of Classis in this new country, the Rev. Michaelius himself summoned the people to a convocation. He examined their certificates, heard their confessions of faith and supervised the election of their church officers. This Consistory was composed of himself as moderator (minister), Peter Minuit and Jan Huyck as elders and Bastiaen Kroll as deacon. The Rev. Jonas Michaelius declared the church an organized body with a minister, two elders and one deacon, according to the Dutch Reformed Church order. He then administered the sacrament of the Lord's Supper to a group of fifty people. Thus began what is believed to be the oldest church organization with an unbroken existence in this country. This was on August 11, 1628.

The first meeting place was in the spacious loft of a horsemill belonging to Francoix Molenmaecher, and in its tower were hung bells brought from Puerto Rico. This served as a place of worship until the arrival in 1633 of a new Director General, Walter van Twiller.

With him came the second minister, the Rev. Everardus
Bogardus, and Adam Roelandson, the first schoolmaster
of New Amsterdam. The loft over the mill was now
replaced by the first church building "like a barn"
down near the East River at what is now 39 Pearl Street.
This building was very plain and probably did not
present an attractive appearance. It served its purpose
until William Kieft became the third Director General
of the colony in 1638.

It was in 1638 that the Rev. Bogardus was united in
marriage to the official nurse of the colony, the widow
Anneke Jans Roeloff. Dr. Hans Kierstede, the physician
of the colony, married her daughter, Sara Roeloff. It
happened that at the marriage of the minister's step-
daughter, when the guests at the wedding and the
Director General himself had become quite merry with
the festivities of the occasion, it was seriously proposed
to, or by, Director Kieft that subscriptions for a new
"suitable and appropriate" church building be taken
then and there. In high spirits the Director General
headed the list with a generous subscription and others
followed at his urging, some it has been said subscrib-
ing amounts which on after and soberer thought, they
had cause to regret. There is no record, however, that
any of these subscriptions were defaulted. The church
building which was erected as a result, stood within
the fort, and the corner-stone was inscribed in Dutch
and reads, as translated, "In the year of our Lord 1642,
William Kieft, Director General, caused the congregation to build this Temple." These were the small be-

ginnings from which the Reformed Church in America has grown.

The old fort occupied the site of the Battery at the foot of Broadway and the church within its walls was called the Church of St. Nicholas or the Church in the Fort. The structure was built of stone, 72 feet long, 50 feet wide and 16 feet high. Its cost was 2,500 guilders, about one thousand dollars.

By 1664 the town of New Amsterdam, which was situated entirely south of Wall Street, had increased in population to about fifteen hundred. People had come to the new country from all parts of Europe, and it has been recorded that as many as eighteen languages were spoken in the colony and that all creeds were tolerated.

At this time King Charles II of England sent a small fleet into the harbor of New Amsterdam and arbitrarily demanded the surrender of the colony to the crown of England. Governor Stuyvesant, taken by surprise and with totally inadequate defense, offered no resistance, and the province of New Netherland passed without a blow into the hands of the English. In 1673, in the course of a war between England and Holland, the Dutch regained possession of the province, but in 1674 it was finally surrendered to the English by treaty.

King Charles gave the province to his brother James, Duke of York, and the name of the province as well as that of the town on Manhattan Island was changed to New York.

During the next hundred years political and social tensions caused considerable anxiety throughout the American colonies. During this period, however, the Reformed Dutch Church in America continued to be under the authority of the Amsterdam Classis of Holland. In 1772, this connection was broken and the church in America became independent and self-governing.

Hardly had the church secured its freedom from foreign ecclesiastical control when the storm of the American Revolution broke over the land. Incidents like the passing of the Stamp Act, the Golden Hill incident, the imposition of a tax on glass, the embargoes laid on trade, the Boston Massacre, the Boston Tea Party and the skirmishes at Lexington and Concord are some of the well-known steps which led to the Revolution. Not so well known, however, is the fact that secret instructions had been sent to Governors in New England and New York with reference to the supplanting of all churches in the colonies by the Church of England. To offset this influence, "Committees of Safety" and "The Sons of Liberty" were organized by the colonists many years before the War of the Revolution was actually started.

The Dutch Church and its ministers were almost without exception aligned with the patriot cause. Of its forty-four ministers only four were known to belong to the Tory ranks. The others held together the Reformed congregations composed of those who were compelled to remain in New York during the conflict. There resulted an unbroken and continuous history of the Reformed Church from the days of Michaelius to the present time.

During this conflict, church buildings in the areas occupied by British soldiers were desecrated. The new Dutch church in New York was used first as a prison and later as a riding academy. The furniture of the churches was frequently carried away to England. The pulpit of one of the New York churches was found many years later in London. The church at New Brunswick, New Jersey, was used as a stable and later as a hospital. Several other buildings were burned to the ground.

When the war was over, the churches faced a serious time of reconstruction. A new form of civil government was being devised, and policies affecting various relationships were being established.

The Dutch people were keen, high-minded and of as great culture as any colonists who came to America at any time. They brought here a genius for organized and representative government, a passion for religion and education, and a tolerance for the religious opinions and prejudices of others, which was of as fine a type as that of the famous William Penn who, in 1682, established the colony of Pennsylvania in accord with the principles of religious tolerance and peace advocated by the Society of Friends.

It was natural, however, that among so many articulate leaders there would be considerable divergence of views with regard to church government. Bitter controversy, even within the churches, existed for several years. It was a trying time for the Dutch church.

Eventually, a way for peace within the churches was opened through the ministry of Dr. John Henry Livingston of Rutgers College at New Brunswick, New Jersey. Dr. Livingston was born at Livingston Manor near Poughkeepsie, New York, was graduated from Yale University, then went to Europe to take his doctor's degree from the University of Utrecht. While in Holland, he kept in touch with American affairs, and felt that he might be able to prepare a plan of peace and union for the American churches.

Upon his return, Dr. Livingston made a notable contribution to the church in the formulation of the Constitution adopted in 1791. In the discussions attendant upon the preparation and adoption of this historic document, his wisdom, genius and ability, as well as his courtesy, tact and dignity, finally resulted in the adoption of the plan of organization under which the church functions today. It is a truly representative form of government, which may be found more fully described in the Appendix of this volume.

As the population of the little town of New York grew, and settlers established themselves on farms in the surrounding country, the church formed new congregations. The earliest Reformed Church in Westchester was located at Fordham in 1696. Next was the Old Dutch Church at Sleepy Hollow, Tarrytown. This building was erected by Frederick Philipse, Lord of the Manor of Philipsburg, in 1697. Services are still held

13

upon occasion in this old church, and the original silver communion service may be seen upon request. Lord Philipse's castle still stands directly across the Albany Post Road from the church.

A century passed before other Dutch churches were established in the county. The first was at Unionville, now Hawthorne, in 1819; and still later, in 1842 the church at Greenville, Town of Greenburg, came into being.

Eight years later, the Bronxville church was organized.

CHAPTER II

THE CHURCH IN BRONXVILLE
1850 - 1920

WHEN the nineteenth century had reached its half-way mark, Bronxville, then known as Under-hill's Crossing, was a community of prosperous farms together with the homes of a few New York business men. They had moved their families away from the noise and dust of the city to the quiet and healthful countryside, to enjoy its beauty. They hoped, too, to escape the yearly epidemics of cholera and yellow fever which took a heavy toll of the city dwellers.

One of the first of these was Alexander Masterton, Sr., who came in 1835 and built his home on the White Plains Road. This is now known as the Dusenberry

15

Place, the home of his granddaughter, Miss Amie S. Dusenberry. The house and grounds remain today practically as he left them when he passed away in 1859, except that a wing was added to the house a few years ago. Mr. Masterton's business interest was in the marble quarries at Tuckahoe.

James M. Prescott, another Bronxville pioneer, built his home in 1840, a large stone manor house on Prescott Avenue in Lawrence Park where the Prescott family resided until 1890 when the estate was sold to William V. Lawrence. It is now the residence of his son, Dudley B. Lawrence.

James P. Swain, Mr. Prescott's son-in-law, acquired a large tract of land which lay along the Bronx River, the lake and the hillside, now Armour Villa Park. In 1842 he built the large stone house which was later converted into one of Bronxville's first apartment houses, Stoneleigh, one of the Alger Court group fronting on Pondfield Road West, formerly Swain Street. Mr. Prescott and Mr. Swain conducted a prosperous ship chandlery business in New York, and later Mr. Swain erected a factory for the manufacture of cutlery on the site of the old Underhill grist and saw mill. This building which is on Pondfield Road West where it crosses the Bronx River, is now occupied as headquarters of the Westchester County Parkway Police Dept.

Skilled factory workers were induced to come here from Sheffield, England, to work at the cutlery factory. These English people with their families, together with the families of the Scottish stone cutters at the Tuckahoe quarries, caused a notable increase in the population of the little settlements.

The railroad was put through in 1844 and a little later a station was established at Underhill's Crossing. In 1847, the Government established a post office at Tuckahoe, and everyone in this area was obliged to go there for his mail.

The nearest places of worship were old St. Paul's in Eastchester, six miles south, and St. John's in Colonial Heights, Tuckahoe, both Episcopal churches; the Asbury Methodist Church in Crestwood, and the Greenville Dutch Reformed Church in the town of Greenburg, five miles to the north. This Reformed Church had been dedicated in 1842 and its first pastor was the Rev. Victor Mareau Hulbert. In 1845, he was succeeded by the Rev. Abel T. Stewart, who was a scholarly man and an exceptionally able preacher. His was the church most favored by the residents of Underhill's Crossing.

At about this time there began to be considerable discussion in favor of a change of name for the village. Mr. James P. Swain is credited with having suggested the present one. When the Government established a post office here in July, 1852, the name Bronxville became official. (See the Appendix for further comment on the name).

Early in the year 1848, Mr. Masterton called on Mr. Prescott and Mr. Swain and said to these two gentlemen, "If you can persuade the Rev. Mr. Stewart, pastor of the Greenville Church, to come to Bronxville and

17

preach once every Sunday, and if a church building is erected here, I will agree to donate the use of my oxen and the labor of some of my men and will give as much of my own time as I can spare in supervising the construction of the building." Mr. Prescott and Mr. Swain agreed to see Mr. Stewart at once and make the proposal. With a Scotsman from Forfar, a Yankee of Puritan ancestry from Connecticut and a Green Mountain boy from Vermont behind the project, success seemed to be assured. Mr. Stewart agreed to the proposal, and on May 23, 1848 the Rev. Thomas DeWitt, D.D., pastor of the Collegiate Reformed Church of New York, and the Rev. James B. Hardenbergh, representing the Classis of New York, visited Bronxville and not only gave their approval but encouraged the committee to the extent of offering outside aid if necessary.

The Rev. Robert Bolton, rector of St. Paul's Episcopal Church in the southern part of Westchester, had purchased the old Lancaster Underhill farm between 1830 and 1835. The farm extended along both sides of Pondfield Road, then known as Underhill Road, and along the present Midland Avenue to the Bronx River. The pre-Revolutionary farm house stood where Meadow Avenue intersects Pondfield Road and south of it was the little knoll which the committee had agreed upon as an ideal location for a church. The Rev. Mr. Bolton was informed of the plan and he generously agreed to donate the plot of about two acres for the proposed building. Mr. Bolton sailed for England shortly thereafter and left the final business arrangements to be handled by his son, the Rev. Cornelius Winter Bolton, who had been appointed trustee to manage the family affairs in the absence of his father. Mr. Robert Bolton died in Cheltenham, England, in 1857 and never saw the little white church on the hill overlooking the pond field. The donor's name has been perpetuated by the group of houses known as Bolton Gardens, which cluster closely to the north of the church on property that was originally a part of the old Underhill farm which had been acquired by the Rev. Robert Bolton.

On February 26, 1849 a deed was delivered to "The Rev. Abel T. Stewart, minister of the Gospel," transferring the knoll to him as minister of the proposed new church, the consideration being "object hereinafter stated and of one dollar." The deed contains the following stipulations: "This conveyance being made however for the purpose of furnishing a site for a place of worship for a Dutch Reformed Society, the buildings and burying ground appertaining thereto, and for no other purpose whatsoever; and which church is to be erected within two years from the date hereof, and in default thereof this conveyance is to be void and the said premises are to revert to the said parties of the first part. Signed: Cornelius Winter Bolton, Trustee."

True to his promise, Mr. Masterton pooled his oxen and carts with those of Mr. Prescott and Mr. Swain. Yokes of oxen hooked up to heavy two-wheeled carts might be seen slowly plodding over the winding roads, hauling lumber, stone and other building material from the town dock in Eastchester Creek to the site of the church. Busy men excavated and graded, fitted the foundation stones and framed the beams, while the entire community cooperated cordially in the undertaking.

Many contributions were made toward the furnishings for the church. The pews came from the Old Middle Dutch Church, formerly located on Nassau Street. This church had been built in 1729 and was used as a prison by the British after the Battle of Long Island. In 1844 it became a United States post office and was so used until 1875. The pews from the Old Middle Dutch Church had been saved by the Collegiate Dutch Reformed Church of New York City and were presented by it to the Bronxville church. They were shipped by sloop from New York to the Town Dock in Eastchester. Lancaster O. Underhill, grandson of the former owner of Underhill farm, and first Bronxville postmaster, loaned his oxen and cart to transport the pews from the dock to their destination. One of the pews, marked with a brass plate, has been preserved and may be seen in the present church.

THE REV. ABEL T. STEWART

ON April 9, 1850 the church was dedicated with impressive services, the Rev. Abel T. Stewart officiating. It was a day of rejoicing and good fellowship. The church was crowded to the doors. It was a plain little building in which this congregation assembled, severe in its lines after the fashion of the New England churches, but in its very simplicity there was beauty, beauty of the spirit within. Upon the following Sunday, Mr. Stewart entered formally upon his ministry in a dual capacity as pastor of the Greenville and Bronxville churches, conducting services in Greenburg each Sunday morning and in Bronxville each Sunday afternoon.

On November 5, 1850 the church was formally organized as a Reformed Protestant Dutch Church by a committee of the Classis of New York, consisting of the Rev. John V. N. Schenck, and Abraham Storm and Charles Dusenberry, elders of the Greenville Church, who met with the congregation on that occasion. The following persons were then received into membership in the church: Mrs. Euphenus Masterton, mother of Alexander, Jr.; Mrs. Jane Morison, mother of Euphenus; Mary Morison, daughter of Jane; Mrs. Catharine Masterton Welbasky, niece of Alexander Masterton, Sr.; Alexander Masterton, Jr.; James P. Swain and Catharine E. Swain, his wife, on certificate from the Greenville Church; James M. Prescott and Ann R. Prescott, his wife; Ellen M. Prescott on certificate from the Duane Street Presbyterian Church in New York; Edward R. Hunt on certificate from the Reformed Dutch Church of Yonkers, New York; and Margaret Harper on confession of faith. In the old church register, following the name of Margaret Harper is written the single word "unknown."

The names of the twelve founders are inscribed on a marble tablet in the narthex of the present church.

At this meeting of organization on November 5, 1850, the first election of officers of the church was

21

held, resulting in the choice of James M. Prescott and James P. Swain as elders, and Edward R. Hunt and Alexander Masterton, Jr., as deacons to serve for one and two years respectively. Their names were published on three successive Sundays as persons elected to office, after which they were ordained as the Consistory of the church by the Rev. Mr. Stewart.

The first meeting of the Consistory was held at the home of Mr. Prescott on Thursday evening, December 14, 1850. At this meeting Alexander Masterton, Jr., was elected clerk and treasurer. He served the church as clerk faithfully until the day of his death, May 3, 1899, just short of a half century. He also served as a deacon for eleven years and as an elder for thirty-seven years and ten months. He served as treasurer from 1850 to 1873 when Francis Bacon succeeded him to that office, which he held for twenty years.

At the meeting on December 14, 1850 the church was formally incorporated with the name, "The Reformed Protestant Dutch Church of Bronxville." The corporate seal shows an open Bible surrounded by a circle, in turn surrounded by another circle in which space is inscribed: "Reformed Protestant Dutch Church, Bronxville, N. Y." The corporate papers were signed by Josiah S. Mitchell and the certificate of incorporation was recorded June 23, 1851 by Albert Lockwood, County Judge.

Now that the church building was completed and occupied, it became necessary to provide shelter for numerous vehicles and horses, with which people from a distance drove to services — so horse sheds were built at the rear of the south side of the hill, and hitching rails installed to which to tether the horses. These sheds remained standing until the new church was built.

On the gently sloping north side, a little burying ground was laid out where "each person who has contributed or shall contribute the sum of fifty dollars or more towards the erection of this church edifice be entitled to a lot for burial, and that such disposal of lots cease with the church debt." During the following decade or two, some sixty interments were made in the little church yard cemetery. For the greater part, the deceased were children of the workers in the factory and the stone quarry, who had died of cholera or some other epidemic which in the early days swept through the community. In 1924 there were only two grave stone markers and a few small mounds to indicate where these loved ones had been interred. When the new church was built, the two stones were placed near the west wall, and the names of the persons buried in the church yard were inscribed on a marble tablet placed in the church floor directly in front of the pulpit.

When the small white church was built, a debt of $1,750 had been incurred upon which interest had to be paid. In order to clear this debt, for payment of which the creditors were pressing, the Consistory was obliged to borrow money. Accordingly on June 1, 1852 a mortgage for $1,750 was made to Nathaniel Valentine, a large property owner in the vicinity and friendly to the church.

23

The first sexton of the church, at a salary of $25 a month, was a Mr. Scott, a stone cutter by trade, who lived in a small house located where Pondfield Court now stands. His son, James, brought up in the Sunday School, learned the trade of a blacksmith, and finally became a minister of the Gospel.

The Rev. Abel T. Stewart had served both the Greenville and Bronxville churches for two years and during his pastorate the Bronxville membership had been increased by thirty-four. In July, 1852, Mr. Stewart resigned to accept a call to the First Reformed Church of Tarrytown.

THE REV. JOSEPH A. COLLIER

IN the summer of 1852 the Rev. Joseph A. Collier was called as the pastor to the two churches, succeeding Mr. Stewart. This relationship existed until 1854, at which time the Consistory decided the church was strong enough to have its own pastor. This was cordially agreed to by the Greenville church with an expression of gratification at the prosperity of the Bronxville church. It was arranged that after the first of April, 1855, Mr. Collier should be exclusively the pastor at Bronxville. This arrangement lasted for only a couple of months, however, because in June he received and accepted a call to a church in Geneva, N. Y. During Mr. Collier's pastorate, eleven communicants were added to the congregation, bringing the total membership to fifty-seven.

THE REV. WASHINGTON ROOSEVELT

TWO YEARS passed before the church again had a regular pastor. During this time services were conducted regularly, if not by an ordained minister, then by one of the elders and there were some accessions to the church membership. The Rev. Washington Roosevelt had been the supply preacher for one year when on October 10, 1857 he was given a call to the ministry of the church. Mr. Roosevelt resided in Pelham and was well acquainted with the families in lower Westchester. He served for sixteen years as minister of the church, driving with his horse and buggy the four miles to and from his home. The church grew steadily during Mr. Roosevelt's ministry and eighty-one persons were added to the church rolls.

During his ministry, too, an effort was made in 1863 to pay off the indebtedness of the church which amounted to $2,500, consisting of the mortgage given to Nathaniel Valentine on June 1, 1852 and accrued interest which had accumulated over the years. An application was made to the Collegiate Church of New York for help. This was granted to the amount of $300 but was not a gift. On the payment of the money the Consistory was required to give a mortgage with certain limitations, leaving a balance of $2,250 still to be paid. On April 29, 1864 this balance was liquidated through the instrumentality of the Masterton family.

It was not until thirty-four years later, during Dr. Webster's pastorate, that the church raised by subscription $300 to liquidate the bond and mortgage given by the Collegiate Church in New York in 1864. The Consistory of the Collegiate Church generously waived the accrued interest.

The little church on the hill had been built with a belfry, but until 1872 no sound had issued from it. Then it was, that Miss Jeanette Chambers, the daughter of James Chambers who lived at "Crow's Nest," gathered her Sunday School class about her and suggested a secret plan. After many months of preparation, during which time each child had worn a badge inscribed with the cryptic letters "N. F.", it was announced that there would be a fair held at "Crow's Nest" and that articles would be sold and the secret of the "N. F.'s" would be disclosed. The day arrived and Bronxville families turned out in large numbers. The sale was a great success. It was then made known that "N. F." meant "Nimble Fingers" and that the money raised was to purchase a bell for the church belfry. The proceeds were sent to the bell foundry at Troy, N. Y., and soon a deep-toned bell arrived having the following inscription: "Presented to the R. D. Church of Bronxville by the N. F.'s." For two generations this bell rang out its musical calls to the congregation, and now hangs in the church tower alongside the chime of bells installed in memory of Otis Tiffany Barnes, one of the most beloved ministers of the church.

On July 10, 1872 the Rev. Mr. Roosevelt wrote a formal letter to the Consistory asking for a dissolution of his pastorate to take effect on the coming October

10th. Mr. Roosevelt stated that because of his advancing age and the distance of his home from the church, he felt unable to discharge his pastoral duties with satisfaction to himself or his church. His resignation was accepted and the church was again without a minister.

THE REV. ALFRED E. MYERS

ON December 11, 1872 the Consistory extended a call to the Rev. Alfred E. Myers, who had served as pastor of Bethany Chapel in Brooklyn, and had just returned from a trip to the Holy Land.

At this time, the Consistory decided that the minister should reside in the community. There was a house available on the road to Tuckahoe, now Sagamore Road, located on the northeast corner of that road and Prescott Avenue, where Hammond House now stands. This house was secured as a parsonage and Mr. Myers, with his young bride, became the first resident minister in Bronxville. Later the house became the property of Col. Alfred E. Latimer.

During the winter of 1872 Bronxville was plagued by numerous small robberies. Homes were entered at night or in the absence of the owners and articles of clothing, silverware and jewelry disappeared systematically. The thieves were not caught and everyone became apprehensive. Even the church did not escape. One Sunday morning, upon opening the church door, the sexton could not believe his eyes. The church carpets were gone and everything of value, including the silver baptismal font, had been removed. After this robbery the thieves disappeared and were never apprehended.

About a year later, in 1873, a Sunday School addition was made to the church, the gift of Alexander Masterton, Jr., in memory of his two sons Joseph Earl and Alexander, both of whom had died in childhood. It was during the erection of this addition, when the carpenters opened the gable of the church roof to join the two buildings, that the mystery of the robberies of 1872 was in part solved. In the attic of the church, reached by a movable ladder and directly over the pulpit, the workmen discovered a cosy little space equipped with a stove, cooking utensils, beds and a full set of burglar's tools. Evidently it was the headquarters of a band of looters. Another mystery was solved by this discovery. Several times during the past few years, members of the congregation had claimed that they had detected the odor of coffee during the morning service. Although at the time they had been laughed at, they had been right. The attic tenants had been preparing Sunday breakfast!

On July 10, 1874 James Minot Prescott, elder, one of the founders of the church, passed away. He had been the first Sunday School Superintendent and was a leader in the parish up to the time of his death at the age of seventy-seven.

The Rev. Mr. Myers was a scholarly man who had served the church well for four years, when he received and accepted a call to a church in Owasco, New York.

THE REV. JOHN HUTCHINS

FOR some years after the ministry of Mr. Roosevelt, there was a succession of short pastorates beginning with Mr. Myers. The church was not large, the community was sparsely settled and there was only a small growth in the church membership.

Mr. Myers was succeeded in July, 1876 by a young Englishman, the Rev. John Hutchins. This was his first charge, and being a young man, he was particularly successful with the young people. There was an increase in Sunday School and church attendance and during his six years as minister of the church there were forty-one additions to the membership.

On May 12, 1879, a brother of Alexander Masterton, Sr., John M. Masterton and his wife Josephine granted and conveyed to the Consistory a plot of land on the northeast corner of what is now Elm Rock Road and Studio Lane. Steps were taken at once to erect a parsonage. The congregation contributed generously and the building was completed without any debt. Mr. Hutchins was the first minister to occupy the Manse. Because of its distance from the church, this property was eventually sold, and was for many years the residence of Harry D. Nims and his family.

From the year 1878 until the fall of 1885 a mission was conducted and supported by the church. This was in a small white school house built in 1835 at Union Corners where New Rochelle Road crosses California Road. James Chambers, member of the Consistory, had special charge of this work. Every Sabbath Day afternoon services were held, a Sunday School maintained, and regular midweek prayer meetings were conducted by members of Consistory, among whom special mention should be made of Alexander Masterton, Jr. In 1884 Mr. Chambers and his family moved to Morristown, New Jersey, and the next year the mission was discontinued and the building sold. It was said of Mr. Chambers that "he faithfully visited the poor, provided clothing and provisions for families in need, and found work for the unemployed," true evidence of his fine spiritual leadership.

Mr. Hutchins resigned on March 31, 1882 to accept a call from the Reformed Church at Ellenville, Ulster County, New York.

The Rev. Edward J. Runk

AFTER another short interval, on November 9, 1882, the Rev. Edward J. Runk was installed as pastor. Soon after his ordination he was married in the church. His wife died a few months later, and the gray marble baptismal font which is still in use was given as a memorial to her. Mr. Runk's pastorate lasted for only two years, and during that time ten persons united with the church. His ministry ended April 1, 1884.

About this time, robbers again broke into the church, and once more the carpets were stolen. In removing them, the marble font was overturned and the base slightly chipped.

Two years followed, during which time the church

was without a regular pastor, but during that time no service was omitted either in church or in Sunday School.

The Rev. John Joseph Rankin

On May 18, 1886 the Rev. John Joseph Rankin, who had served the church as stated supply during the previous six months, was duly installed as pastor. Mr. Rankin remained with the church for two years, until March, 1888 when because of failing eyesight he was obliged to retire. Four new members joined the church during his term.

From March, 1888 until December, 1890 the church was again without an ordained leader. These were difficult years for the church, but due to the wise administration of the Consistory and the devotion of a few families, willing and able, the work of the church was continued uninterruptedly. In August, 1889 Francis Bacon was ordained as an elder and eight new members were added to the roll.

The Rev. Peter MacQueen

On December 10, 1890 the Rev. Peter MacQueen came as a stated supply and was so well liked that he was duly installed as minister on May 14, 1891. Peter MacQueen was an eloquent speaker and people came from miles around to hear him. It is related that he often walked over to the Bacon property, where he would sit under the grape arbor writing poetry to be used in his Sunday sermons. He made friends easily and his

31

dry Scotch humor was recalled years after he left for larger fields.

At this time there were only about forty families in the church. The names of Masterton, Smith, Swain, Hay, Crittenden, Imrie, Prescott, Burwell, Underhill, Cox, Latimer, Burtnett, DeWitt, Kraft, Bacon, Dusenberry, Sprenger, Chambers and Ferris stand out as the ones who were most active in church work.

Thirteen persons joined the church during Mr. Mac-Queen's two years of ministry. On April 10, 1893 he resigned to become the pastor of a large church in Somerville, Massachusetts.

The Rev. J. Hendrick DeVries

A few weeks later, on May 21, Consistory extended a call to the Rev. J. Hendrick DeVries who was a native of Holland, the only real "Dutchman" to fill the pulpit of Bronxville's Dutch Church. During his four years in the church twelve names were added to the roll. He retired on January 11, 1897 to become minister in the Second Presbyterian Church of Princeton, New Jersey.

The Rev. William S. C. Webster, D.D.

On September 15, 1897 the Rev. Dr. William S. C. Webster was installed and continued in office for six busy years, during which occurred several events worthy of note.

In 1899, Frank R. Chambers came to reside at "Crow's Nest," the former home of James Chambers. The church school had become overcrowded by this time, due to the fact that many people were moving to Bronxville to occupy homes in the new developments of Lawrence Park and Armour Villa Park. Not long after their arrival in Bronxville, Mr. and Mrs. Frank R. Chambers generously built a much needed addition to the church school and presented it to the church in memory of their young son, William Waller Chambers, who had recently died. The addition consisted of a primary room with a great stone fireplace, and an office and a kitchen equipped with a gas stove and modern conveniences. With these added facilities, the church became a center for many and varied social activities.

On May 2, 1899 Alexander Masterton, Jr., passed away. Many tributes were paid to the memory of Mr. Masterton. He was respected, honored and loved by all. By his last will and testament, Mr. Masterton left to the church two thousand dollars to be invested and held as a permanent endowment, one half of the income to be devoted to the church school and the other half for the benefit of the church. In tribute to his memory, nine memorial windows were placed in the church. A few years later, Mrs. William Nelson Ferris, his daughter, presented on behalf of herself and her children two brass collection plates in memory of her father and mother. These are still in use.

The fiftieth anniversary of the church was celebrated on Sunday, November 11, 1900 by special jubilee services. Taking part in these were Dr. Webster, the Rev. John Hutchins and Frank R. Chambers. On Monday the women of the church gave an afternoon reception in the church parlors, and in the evening a meeting was addressed by the Rev. Dr. John K. Allen, president of the Westchester Classis, and several former ministers of the church were also present.

At the Annual Meeting held October 8, 1902 Francis Bacon, because of ill health, presented his resignation to the Consistory. He had faithfully served first as deacon and later as elder since October 9, 1873, and had held the office of treasurer for a period of nearly twenty years. Mr. Bacon passed away December 20, 1905 and by his death the church lost one of its most devoted members.

The mahogany communion table used in the old church had been given in his memory and when the present church was erected it was replaced by his family, as a continuing memorial to Mr. Bacon, by the larger Gothic oak table which is now in use.

Frank R. Chambers was elected to fill the vacancy caused by the resignation of Francis Bacon, thus beginning his long career as an outstanding leader in church affairs.

Since 1851 the church had been using at its services of Holy Communion the silver service presented by the Masterton family. In 1903, Consistory voted to adopt the use of individual communion cups, at that time being generally used elsewhere, and the required number of small glass cups was purchased.

On May 8, 1903, Dr. Webster presented his resignation and was formally dismissed by Classis on June 30,

CHURCH IN 1873 SHOWING SUNDAY SCHOOL ADDITION

INTERIOR OF THE CHURCH IN 1873

1903. He had faithfully served the church for six years and brought into its membership seventy-two persons.

THE REV. JAMES LOVEJOY ROBERTSON, D.D.

AFTER the retirement of Dr. Webster, there were a few months when the church seemed dormant. However, Mr. Chambers had kept the Sunday School active.

At this time, the Rev. Dr. James Lovejoy Robertson was living in Yonkers in retirement because of failing health. He had had a wide experience in the ministry, having been pastor of large and influential churches in Cleveland and Cincinnati, Ohio; in Geneva, Rochester and Cortland, New York; and in Galveston, Texas. He regained his health and became eager to take up active service again. Having learned that the Reformed Church in Bronxville was without a pastor, he called upon Mr. Chambers and asked the privilege of having the church opened for Sunday evening services. He did not wish any compensation, but desired an opportunity to preach the word of God.

The request was granted. The opening service was attended by fourteen people.

In a short time there was a congregation of nearly two hundred. Dr. Robertson was appointed a stated supply by Classis, and on December 9, 1903 was duly called and on April 17, 1904 was installed as minister of the church. From the very beginning of his ministry, the work of the church prospered. He speedily won the affection of the people and the membership increased rapidly.

35

In January, 1904 it was felt that the parsonage on
Elm Rock Road was too far distant from the church
and not sufficiently commodious for Dr. Robertson's
large family. The Consistory decided to sell it and erect
a new parsonage on a site nearer the church. The sum
received from the sale was not enough to purchase a plot
and build a home. This difficulty was overcome through
the generosity of Mr. and Mrs. Frank R. Chambers who
granted and conveyed to the church the plot of land on
the southwest corner of Pondfield Road and Midland
Avenue, directly across the avenue from the church.

A building committee consisting of Frank R. Chambers, elder, and Elias W. Dusenberry, deacon, was
appointed to engage an architect and submit plans for
the proposed building. The plans were submitted to
Consistory in April, 1904. At that time, Mr. Dusenberry
reported that he had entered into a contract with Mr.
Chambers who had agreed to erect the new parsonage
for the sum appropriated for the purpose, and upon the
land mentioned above. The work proceeded rapidly
and the following December Dr. Robertson and his
family took possession of their new home.

Frederick W. Kraft, owner of the Piano and Glove
Leather Factory that stood on the land now occupied
by Midland Gardens, owned a narrow strip of land
between the church and Midland Avenue. In November, 1904 Mr. Kraft presented a deed of this strip to
the church. The Consistory, in an appropriate resolution passed at the December meeting, thanked Mr.
Kraft "for this kindly gift to the Church."

Alterations to the church building had been long discussed, and in January, 1906 plans were completed to go forward with the work. The gallery in the east end of the church, where the original organ had been installed, was removed. A new, commodious alcove to house a new organ and to accommodate a choir was built at the north side of the front of the church. The Ladies' Aid Society raised funds for the new pipe organ installed here, but the money necessary for the substantial improvements, repairs and alterations was obtained by subscription from the people of the church.

The roof was reshingled and other necessary repairs made. The old pews, which had come from the Old Middle Dutch Church in New York some fifty years before, were taken out and new ones installed. These were white with mahogany trim. A few of them may be seen in the corridors of the present Bible School. A new pulpit was provided and the entire interior of the church was redecorated.

In 1907, a grandson of Alexander Masterton, Sr., Elias W. Dusenberry, who had been a deacon since 1899, was elected and installed as an elder. From that time until he passed away in October, 1948 in the 87th year of his age, Mr. Dusenberry, in addition to his wise counsel in the Consistory, rendered an outstanding service to the church. Fresh flowers in season from his garden at the old homestead on White Plains Road or from the Chambers garden graced the pulpit each Sunday. In Winter the flowers came from the Chambers' greenhouse. Mr. Dusenberry's arrangements were re-

37

markably beautiful and for many years lent an added distinction to the beauty of the church service.

During the twelve years of Dr. Robertson's pastorate, 205 persons were added to the membership of the church. There were 50 dismissals and 21 deaths, leaving a total membership in 1915 of 247. Of the 205 new members, 111 were on confession of faith, indicative of the excellent work accomplished in the Church School under the superintendence of Frank R. Chambers, in bringing young people into the church.

It was during this period that Mr. Chambers purchased an old omnibus, named by the children "The Gospel Coach," to collect the boys and girls on stormy Sundays and transport them to Sunday School.

In 1914, an interesting new venture was undertaken in the institution of evening Finnish church services for the numerous Finnish people in the vicinity, many of whom were employed in the homes of Bronxville and neighboring communities. Some mid-week social gatherings were also sponsored by the Women's Society of the church. The preaching was in charge of Finnish clergymen, one of the prominent men engaged in this work being the Rev. Kalle MaKinen, pastor of the "Finnish Seaman's Mission Church" in Brooklyn, New York.

During the last five years of Dr. Robertson's ministry, the church was fortunate in being able to obtain as an occasional preacher and assistant to Dr. Robertson, the Rev. Dr. Louis M. Sweet. Dr. Sweet lived in Mount Vernon and was a member of the staff of the

Biblical Seminary in New York. He was a friend of many members of the congregation. After Dr. Robertson's resignation, Dr. Sweet acted as stated supply until a new minister was called.

On the sixteenth of June, 1915 Dr. Robertson, who was now seven years beyond his "three score and ten" years of age, presented his resignation, to take effect in the coming Fall. There was genuine sadness in the church and community when on January 4, 1916, Dr. Robertson suddenly passed away.

The Rev. Otis Tiffany Barnes

On February 16, 1916 the Consistory extended a unanimous call to the Rev. Otis Tiffany Barnes, of Chappaqua, New York, where he had served four years as pastor of the Congregational Church. He entered upon his work in the Bronxville Reformed Church on April 1, 1916 and was formally installed as twelfth pastor of the church on June 2, 1916. Mr. Barnes was a scholarly young man whose sterling worth and fine intellect appealed to the older members of the community and whose youth appealed to the young people.

During the Winter of 1916 the Boy Scouts of America organization had come to Bronxville by way of the public school. Hardly had Mr. Barnes taken up his residence in the village, when he was drafted to lead the movement and put it on a sound basis. He was essentially a boy's man and the Scout troop grew rapidly. New patrols were formed and assistant scoutmasters appointed.

Upon Mr. Barnes' death, it was found that he had left a pencil sketch of a proposed Scout Cabin. This was eventually built, given his name and dedicated to his memory. Some years later, the Cabin was greatly enlarged and it is still in active use by the Boy Scouts.

When the United States entered World War I in 1917, all village and church organizations became active in war work. The Reformed Church was busy day and night, assisting the Red Cross, the Y.M.C.A. and Y.W.C.A., doing volunteer nursing during the Spanish Influenza epidemic, and enlisting aid for the Armenian and Syrian Relief Funds, the Belgian and Polish Funds and other agencies for the relief of war sufferers. Substantial contributions were made to these various causes.

Two large American flags, donated by Mr. and Mrs. William F. Kraft, stood on either side of the pulpit. A service flag prepared by the women of the church hung in front of the little white church and is now placed in the nave of the present church.

A bronze Honor Roll, listing the forty names of church members who participated in the conflict, is now in the narthex of the church.

In the spring of 1918, the pastor having expressed his desire to render some service to his country in active war work, the Consistory extended the length of his usual vacation, and Mr. Barnes went to work in the shipyards at Hog Island, Philadelphia. He returned to Bronxville in the Fall, and with the consent of Consistory was preparing to go overseas as a Chaplain in the Army. Before his preparations were completed, the war came to an end.

A special service of Thanksgiving and Dedication led by Mr. Barnes, was held on Sunday morning, November 17, 1918, the first Sunday after the abdication of the Kaiser and the signing of the Armistice between the Allies and Germany.

On Thursday, February 20, 1919, the community was shocked and grieved by the announcement of the death of the Rev. Mr. Barnes. He had been attacked by meningitis, for which at that time there was no known cure, and he had passed away after only three short days of illness.

During Mr. Barnes' three years as minister, 111 names were added to the church rolls and the attendance at both Sunday School and church had grown to such an extent that plans to enlarge the building were being considered.

Bronxville Village was seeing many changes in its civic life. Apartment houses were being erected, increasing the population by leaps and bounds. The fine community spirit so characteristic of the old days was being challenged. The war had left the country unsettled and the church was facing new and serious problems.

During the Spring and Summer of 1919, the church pulpit was again supplied by Dr. Louis M. Sweet.

CHAPTER III

---◆---

THE CHURCH IN BRONXVILLE
1920 - 1950

THE REV. DEANE EDWARDS

IN September, 1919, a call was extended to the Rev. Deane Edwards to become the minister of the church. He assumed his new duties during that month and on January 21, 1920, was regularly installed. He was destined to see more changes during his ministry than had occurred during the entire life of the church for nearly three-quarters of a century.

Mr. Edwards entered upon his work with vigor and as a result there was a steady growth in the church membership. His fine organizing ability made him a leader and an active worker in the Classis of Westchester.

The Bronxville community was growing very fast, particularly in the area lying west of the railroad and the Bronx River. Mr. Edwards, with a keen sense of responsibility and desire for helpfulness, aroused the interest of the people in that area and in due time a small portable chapel, housing only a small Sunday School, was taken over from the Presbyterian Board, moved to a more convenient location at Bronxville Road and Boyd Place, redecorated within and painted without, and on October 10, 1920 was rededicated and became a part of the work of the Reformed Church of Bronxville. This Sunday School continued under the superintendence of Alan R. Fullarton, and Mr. Edwards preached there on Sunday afternoons.

This little chapel was then named "The West Center," and it was represented in Consistory by one elder, Mr. Fullarton, and by one or more deacons. The congregation grew, and two years later, when Dr. Louis M. Sweet became pulpit associate, he and Mr. Edwards preached on alternate Sunday mornings at the Reformed Church on Midland Avenue and the West Center at Boyd Place.

This arrangement continued for four years, until October, 1926 when the Rev. William Thomas Heath became associate minister of the church, his main responsibility being the West Center. This plan was adopted with the understanding that after one year the West Center congregation would be free to form an independent church, with whatever denominational affiliation was desired.

The year proved to be a very successful one, and the group decided to withdraw, to join the Congregational Church and to call the Rev. Mr. Heath as minister. Accordingly, the elders dismissed fifty-one members from the Reformed Church to become charter members of the West Center Congregational Church and transferred by duly executed deed the property purchased at Pondfield Road West and Chatfield Road as a permanent site for a new building. The new church continued to prosper and in the spring of 1929 the congregation moved from the little wooden chapel to a new building erected on Pondfield Road West.

The seventieth anniversary of the Bronxville Church was celebrated on Sunday, November 21, 1920 with appropriate ceremony. A "Birthday Party" had been held on the preceding Wednesday in the church parlors when Charles Ruston, clerk of the church, exhibited and told the story of twenty objects connected with the history of the church. Among them was the first minute book of the elders, and the original certificate of incorporation.

In March, 1921, Jacob Egbert, who had been the treasurer of the church for twenty-five years, resigned. He had been a deacon for many years also, and was one of the most faithful and beloved members of the church.

It became increasingly evident that the Reformed Church building was inadequate for the work it should be doing and the service it should render in the community. The only solution seemed to be a new church. There were many objections, mainly from the old and faithful members for whom the old building held many precious memories. Mr. Edwards dealt with this situation with tact and understanding. During the first years of his ministry he studied the problem, made many friends, grew into the village life and won the confidence of his parish.

On June 7, 1923, a special congregational meeting was called and a resolution was adopted that a "new church should be built as soon as practicable at Pondfield Road and Midland Avenue." Pursuant to this resolution, the following were appointed a building committee: Rolland J. Hamilton, chairman; J. Arthur Singmaster, secretary; Ferris J. Meigs, LaMont A. Warner, Hugh S. Robertson, Frank W. Wilson and Roger A. Young, with Deane Edwards, ex-officio.

A committee on new church requirements consisting of Mr. Warner, Mrs. Charles W. Halsey (the present Mrs. A. L. Warnshuis), Mr. Fullarton and Mr. Edwards had already made a list of necessities which was turned over to the building committee and was eventually placed in the hands of the architects.

The building committee decided that the architect should be chosen by means of an anonymous competition to be conducted according to the rules of the American Institute of Architects.

It was almost a year later, on May 15, 1924, that the committee met with Alexander B. Trowbridge as professional advisor and Prof. William A. Boring of Columbia University as one of the judges. From among the six sets of plans which had been submitted anonymously, it was found, after the choice was made and the seals broken disclosing the names of the contestants, that the winning plan was the work of Harry Leslie Walker of Bronxville. Mr. Walker's plans were later formally approved and accepted by Consistory and the congregation.

A finance committee was appointed, of which Ferris J. Meigs was chairman and Edgar S. Bowling, vice-chairman. This committee was ably assisted by the minister and a large number of volunteer workers.

Pledges of an amount sufficient to warrant beginning construction of the new building were in hand early in November, 1924. Immediately thereafter, the committee and the architect undertook the placing of building contracts, and in February, 1925 the contract for the general construction of the building was awarded to the William L. Crow Construction Company.

Separate contracts were awarded for the lighting fixtures, door hardware, chancel woodwork, pews and the glazing of the windows, all of which work was designed by the architect and fabricated under his direction.

The lighting fixtures and door hardware are of wrought iron, hand-forged upon the anvil in the medieval manner by Samuel Yellin in his shop in Philadelphia. Mr. Yellin, who died a few years ago, was generally acknowledged to be the greatest artist-craftsman in wrought iron in this country. Examples of his work appear in many notable buildings and are exhibited in many art museums. Samuel Yellin won the Philadelphia Award, an annual prize established by Edward W. Bok, to be given to the most notable citizen of Philadelphia of a particular year.

The chancel furnishings were fabricated by Irving and Casson of Boston. All of this work is of solid oak, no veneer being used, and all hand carved; it is cut from the solid block, the carving and panel being in a single piece.

The original windows were of temporary glass, but have now been replaced, except for four in the clerestory, by memorial windows which are described in detail in the chapter on memorials.

Inasmuch as a larger area of ground was needed for the new building than that occupied by the old one, and since this area would include the burial plot, in October, 1924, Consistory took action in accordance with the laws of the State to have all remains removed from the little cemetery at the side of the church. They were reverently placed in a vault built under the nave of the church. An interment ceremony was conducted by the minister, and the vault permanently closed. Inscribed on a marble slab in the floor of the church near the pulpit will be found the names of those whose remains were so interred.

The corner stone of the new church was laid on Sunday, June 21, 1925 with impressive ceremonies. Seated on the platform were the ministers of the church: the Rev. Deane Edwards and Dr. Louis M. Sweet; Professor James Coffin Stout, Superintendent of the Church School; Rolland J. Hamilton, Chairman of the Building Committee; Ferris J. Meigs, Chairman of the Building Campaign Committee; Edgar S. Bowling, Chairman of the Committee on Furnishings; Frank R. Chambers, Senior Member of Consistory; Alan R. Fullarton, Superintendent of the West Center Church School; Miss Amie S. Dusenberry, of the Building Campaign Committee; Mrs. William Nelson Ferris, Mrs. A. G. Burtnett and Miss Augusta Oppendick, three members who had joined the church in the 1860's; and Harry Leslie Walker, the architect of the building.

After the opening exercises, consisting of salutation, the reading of the liturgy and a musical number by the quartette, Mr. Edwards spoke briefly expressing satisfaction at the interest of so many individuals and organizations and then introduced Mr. Hamilton who read the history of the building project. He said, in part, "We build not to satisfy our pride nor to symbolize our prosperity, but we do this work to evidence our faith in the church as an institution, to glorify that faith, and to make it a vital and living thing by creating the physical means for its expression. We build for the present, yes: but still more for our children and our children's children." A list of the contents of the box in the cornerstone, consisting of thirty-one items, was then read by Miss Amie S. Dusenberry. After the final words of the ritual were spoken, the benediction was pronounced.

The seventy-fifth anniversary of the founding of the church was celebrated in November 1925 at a dinner held at the Hotel Gramatan. The program of the evening came to a climax with the introduction of Mr. Bowling, who opened the way for "birthday" gifts toward the furnishing of the church and Bible school rooms. Those present arose to announce their gifts and as each pledge was made, a candle was lighted on the great birthday cake. Many of the contributions came from the various church organizations.

To begin the construction of the new building it was of course necessary to remove the existing one, but it was found that by removing the Sunday School rooms only, the old church could be left standing in what was to be the cloister garden, and so around it on three sides arose the new building. The congregation continued to worship in the old church until the church school auditorium was ready for use. At a final service on April 2, 1926 Mr. Edwards offered this closing prayer: "Oh Thou to whom places as well as people are sacred, we bow in humble farewell to this place which has for many years been Thy sanctuary. We thank Thee for Thy servants who have worshipped in this place and sanctified it by their faith and devotion. We thank Thee for the influence that has gone forth into the world from here. We thank Thee for the larger things to which it has given birth. We pray that the old things may be

a sacred inspiration and the new things a call to larger
Christian faith and devotion. We pray that the new
may join with the old in bringing many sons and
daughters into Thy Kingdom. And now may the grace
of our Lord Jesus Christ, the love of God the Father,
and the communion of the Holy Spirit be with us all.
Amen."

From April 9 until December, Sunday worship services were held in the new church school auditorium.
Consistory met for the first time in the new edifice on
September 17. On November 7, the Founders Tablet,
bearing the names of the twelve charter members, was
formally dedicated in the narthex of the church.

On Monday evening, December 20, a dedication
pageant written by LaMont A. Warner, "Let There Be
Light," was presented. It depicted the history of the
Christian Church from the earliest times and ended
with a dedication ceremony of the new church. There
were six episodes in which 250 persons took part before
a capacity audience.

The first Sunday service in the new church was held
at 11 o'clock in the morning of December 26, 1926 and
was conducted by the Rev. Deane Edwards, who
preached from the text which he had chosen to be inscribed above the main entrance of the church, — the
words of the 43rd Psalm: "O send out Thy light and
Thy truth: let them lead me; let them bring me unto
Thy holy hill, and to Thy tabernacles."

The church was formally dedicated at 3:30 o'clock
on the same day with impressive ceremonies.

THE CHURCH IN 1906

THE CHURCH IN 1926

The preacher of the occasion was the Rev. Malcolm James MacLeod, minister of the Collegiate Church of St. Nicholas of New York, the oldest church with a continuous history in America. He took for his text Matthew 12:6, "One Greater than the Temple is Here." The responsive reading was led by Professor Allen Macy Dulles of Auburn Theological Seminary, father of Mrs. Deane Edwards. The scripture was read by the Rev. William Thomas Heath, associate minister of the church. Mr. Edwards then called upon Harry Leslie Walker, the architect; Rolland J. Hamilton, chairman of the building committee and Frank R. Chambers, senior member of Consistory, to present the building for dedication. Mr. Edwards offered a prayer of dedication, interspersed with responses by the congregation.

The service was concluded with the singing by the chorus choir of Gounod's "Unfold Ye Portals," and a benediction.

Mrs. Francis Bacon, the only living person who had been present seventy-six years before, at the dedication of the church in 1850, was in attendance at this service.

On Sunday, June 19, 1927 a memorial service was held at which time numerous gifts and memorials were dedicated. The bells in the tower, given by Ralph W. Gwinn and family in memory of the Rev. Otis Tiffany Barnes, had been dedicated in the previous November.

On January 1, 1928 Frederick L. Fay was added to the church staff as Director of Religious Education. Five years later he resigned in order to continue his studies in his chosen field.

51

In 1929, occurred the death of Charles Ruston, Sr., at the age of ninety-one. An elder and clerk of Consistory for eight years, he had resigned his offices in 1924, because of failing health. Mr. Ruston had been active in all the work of the church, and was the author of the Church Manual and History written in 1917.The Pulpit Bible now in use was the gift of Mr. Ruston.

In the spring of 1929 Mr. Edwards received a call to the Church in Radburn, Fairlawn, New Jersey and on June 25, he sent a letter "To the Parishioners of the Reformed Church of Bronxville, N.Y." in which he said: "My new work is unusually unique and challenging — an interdenominational pastorate of a kind which, so far as I know, has never before been attempted."

Mr. Edwards' last sermon in Bronxville was preached on Sunday morning, June 30, 1929.

Unsurpassed were the courage, the vision and the organizing ability displayed by Mr. Edwards in developing and establishing the West Center Congregational Church and promoting the building of the new Reformed Church at Pondfield Road and Midland Avenue. The kindness and the unselfish devotion of Mr. an Mrs. Edwards to the church and community left an enduring mark upon the village. The Bronxville Reformed Church under their leadership had increased from a membership of 295 to 659, had become the largest church in the Classis of Westchester, and one of the strongest in the denomination.

At the termination of Mr. Edwards' ministry, Dr. A. L. Warnshuis became moderator and chairman of

Consistory. He served the church in this capacity until the arrival of Dr. Powell. During this interval, the pulpit was supplied by guest preachers, the most frequent of whom was Dr. Louis M. Sweet.

THE REV. JOHN HENDERSON POWELL, JR., PH.D., D.D.

ANOTHER era in the life of the Reformed Church in Bronxville was begun on January 27, 1930 when the Rev. John Henderson Powell, Jr., was called to the ministry of the church. His first sermon was preached on February 9, 1930, before a congregation which filled the church to capacity. A month later, on the afternoon of Sunday, March 9, 1930, he was formally installed as minister at an impressive service in which many Westchester divines participated and which was witnessed by a large congregation.

Early in 1933 the Rev. William H. McCance came to the church as assistant minister. He served until 1938 when he resigned to become the minister of the Congregational Church of Middlebury, Connecticut.

Shortly thereafter, the Rev. Howard C. Shaffer became assistant minister. In 1942 he resigned to accept a call to the pastorate of the Colonial Church (Reformed) at Bayside, Long Island, New York.

The Rev. George A. Ackerly was then appointed associate minister of the church, which office he held until his resignation late in 1949. He thereafter became an assistant minister at the Church of the Covenant at Cleveland, Ohio.

When Dr. Powell came to the Reformed Church in Bronxville in February, 1930 there were 659 resident members. During his twenty years of ministry, 2,262 new members were received into the church, coming from twenty-five different denominations. Accessions to the church reached a high point on April 5, 1936 when one hundred persons were received into membership.

Soon after taking up his work in Bronxville, Dr. Powell rearranged the church roll geographically, dividing the community into four districts. Later, he instituted the present neighborhood organization of the membership committee of the Women's Society to assist with the church calling and thus made the service of the church more available to the life of the community.

Dr. Powell, always generous in his recognition of the value of the Women's Society, felt that all social functions for the church congregation should be under the supervision of the Society, and to this end he advocated a Special Activities Committee of the Women's Society. Also he suggested that a special committee which had been supplying flowers for the chancel each Sunday (after Mr. Dusenberry was no longer able to perform this service, as described before) become one of the regular committees of the Women's Society. Now known as the Church Flower Committee, the scope of its work was expanded to make it possible for memorial flowers to be given, by pre-arrangement for special dates, by members of the congregation.

54

Projects started during Dr. Powell's ministry include the Young People's Society, which was begun on his suggestion in 1931, the Couple's Club and later, after the war, the Young Adult Group for people from twenty to thirty years of age.

Dr. Powell's accomplishment in reorganizing a Men's Club of the church is mentioned in a following chapter. He always took an active part in community affairs and was Chaplain of the Leonard Morange Post of the American Legion.

While in Bronxville, Dr. Powell published a volume of sermons on the Ten Commandments, and contributed several articles to such religious journals as *Christendom* and *Religion in Life*. He represented the Reformed Church in America at the 400th Anniversary of the Reformation, in Geneva, Switzerland in 1936 and the same year at the 300th Anniversary of the founding of the University of Utrecht in Holland. The same summer he was an exchange preacher to Great Britain, preaching in Glasgow and Aberdeen and was a delegate to the World Conference on Faith and Order in Edinburgh, Scotland. In 1948 he was a delegate to the meeting of the Alliances of Reformed Churches in Geneva, Switzerland.

Under Dr. Powell's leadership, the Bronxville church exhibited great patriotism throughout World War II, and served as a focus of numerous activities, not the least of which was the raising of funds for relief work. Large sums were contributed to the Red Cross and various welfare agencies and Dr. Powell devoted many

55

sermons to exhortations to his congregation for an all-out support of the national effort, as well as to discussions of the basic issues of the war.

On V. E. (Victory in Europe) Day, May 6, 1945, special services were held in the church. There was a spontaneous meeting for meditation at four o'clock in the afternoon with prayers and hymns appropriate to the occasion, followed that evening at 8:15 by another service. Prayers and meditation with devotional music by the choir featured this meeting also, and Dr. Powell made a brief address before a large crowd of people which overflowed into the aisles and narthex of the church. On August 14 and 15, 1945, there were V. J. (Victory in Japan) Day services conducted by Mr. Ackerly.

In 1942 the church sold to the village the manse on the corner of Pondfield Road directly across Midland Avenue from the church. This was done at the request of the village authorities in order that the plot occupied by the new Village Hall might be completed. During the war the manse was used by the Home Defense Organization as its headquarters. When hostilities ceased, the building was razed and the property graded to complete the lawn surrounding the Village Hall.

The church at this time was still burdened with a heavy indebtedness as the result of the construction and equipment of the new church edifice. In order to obtain the necessary funds for its completion a mortgage had been placed on the church property, and outstanding loans obtained from the local banks of Bronxville, totaling $140,000. This indebtedness was gradually reduced in comparatively small amounts until 1936 when a campaign was conducted which resulted in discharging the remaining indebtedness of the church to the local banks and reducing by one-third the amount of the mortgage. Later, as the result of a further campaign and by applying the sum realized from the sale of the manse, the entire indebtedness was liquidated.

Dr. Powell instituted a series of special mid-week evening Lenten services in which each year six of the outstanding ministers of the country came to preach at the church during the Lenten season. Large attendance indicated the people's appreciation of the opportunity to hear these men.

The remarkable growth in membership and in attendance during Dr. Powell's ministry was the natural result of his preaching, particularly of his penetrating analysis of the basis of our faith. He stimulated his hearers to ponder deeply upon the fundamental philosophies which underlie the spiritual verities of their beliefs. The purely devotional or spiritual awareness of his congregation was thus developed and made vital, because it was based on intellectual conviction.

He advocated a revision of traditional theology in the light of modern science. He felt strongly that the whole intellectual outlook of the western world had changed completely in the last four hundred years as a result of the discoveries and implications of modern science and that since orthodox theology had been formulated wholly in terms of a pre-scientific outlook, the major need of religion in our time was to bring it up to date, to the end that man might grasp a more adequate and reasonable conception of God and His omnipotence.

He tried to accomplish this not only in his preaching, but in his personal conversations with those who were troubled about their religious faith. Many people joined the church because they found here a twentieth century approach to religion, and some came from other communities to worship because they seemed to appreciate the particular emphasis of Dr. Powell's preaching. He possessed a remarkable ability to express his ideas through effective word pictures, and to portray a personality with vividness and deep insight. He also showed his great respect for the wisdom of the ancient philosophers, and revealed an extraordinary knowledge of Bible history, which he interpreted with clarity in the light of present-day conditions.

Fearless in the expression of his attitudes upon current problems, Dr. Powell expressed his views without equivocation upon such subjects as Pacifism and Modern Education, both secular and religious. His opinions upon these subjects, while not accepted with equal enthusiasm by all of his hearers, were stimulating for discussion.

Dr. Powell's outstanding leadership was in the realm of the intellectual and spiritual. But he aroused the members of his congregation also to a greater sense of their obligation to world wide benevolent enterprises.

While strongly advocating the complete payment of the church indebtedness, which was accomplished as described during his pastorate, it was his constant hope that the budget for benevolence eventually would equal the budget for current expense.

It was the good fortune of the congregation of the church to enjoy a high quality of spiritual leadership during the extended ministry of Dr. John Powell. His eminence in scholarship, originality in thought, intellectual honesty, sincerity of purpose, and his conviction that accepting and following the teachings of Christ is the way to a life of truth, beauty and goodness have been indelibly stamped on the life of the community.

At the morning service on December 24, 1949, Dr. Powell announced to the congregation that he had tendered to the Consistory his resignation as minister of the church to take effect on February 10, 1950, the twentieth anniversary of the beginning of his pastorate. Following this announcement, Thomas B. Gilchrist, president pro tem of Consistory, informed the congregation that Dr. Powell's resignation had been accepted with profound regret.

AN INTERIM PERIOD

FEBRUARY 10, 1950 — SEPTEMBER 10, 1950

THE Rev. Theodore H. Thielpape, pastor of the Crescent Place Reformed Church, Yonkers, New York, was appointed by the Classis of Westchester to serve the Bronxville Reformed Church as moderator during the interim between the termination of Dr. Powell's pastorate and the installation of his successor. This choice of a moderator resulted in a sympathetic and friendly relationship between Mr. Thielpape and the Consistory which materially lightened the burdens resting upon the shoulders of Consistory during the seven months period that the church was without a regular pastor. When the duties of the moderator were terminated by the installation of the new minister, the Consistory expressed deep appreciation of the kindly and neighborly assistance that he had rendered.

Immediately following Dr. Powell's resignation, the Consistory appointed a committee composed of twenty-eight representative men and women of the congregation under the chairmanship of its president pro tem, Thomas B. Gilchrist, to explore the field of eligible ministers and to make a recommendation of their choice to the Consistory. An organization meeting of the committee was held on December 28, 1949 and its task was undertaken with devotion and zeal. Advice and suggestions were sought and obtained from the heads of the leading theological seminaries as well as from members and friends of the church. Months of intensive effort ensued involving extensive correspondence, interviews with candidates and excursions to neighboring and more distant municipalities to listen to the sermons of possible candidates, delivered from the pulpits of their own churches.

During this period the church was fortunate in securing the services of the Rev. Robert R. Bryan, D.D., as interim resident minister. Dr. Bryan at once endeared himself to the congregation by his winning personality, sympathetic understanding and the high quality of his preaching ability. He assumed his duties in February 1950 but was unable to continue for the full term of the interim period because of an engagement in Europe which compelled him to terminate his relationship with the church at the end of June.

Again, the Consistory was fortunate in securing for the balance of the interim period as temporary minister, the services of the Rev. Hugh Baillie MacLean, Ph.D., Professor of the study of the Old Testament at New Brunswick Theological Seminary, who served the church with distinction during the months of July and August.

Late in June the Selection Committee notified the Consistory that, after considering the qualifications of a large number of distinguished ministers, it was prepared to make a report to Consistory. Thereupon it announced its unanimous recommendation that a call be extended to the Rev. Lowell Russell Ditzen, D.D., of the First Presbyterian Church of Utica, N. Y., to become the minister of the Bronxville Reformed Church. The Committee's report was promptly and unanimously approved by Consistory and a call was forthwith issued to Dr. Ditzen.

On July 9th at the morning service, announcement was made that Dr. Ditzen had accepted the call and would conduct his first service in the church on September 10th.

Another major accomplishment by the Consistory during this interim period was the securing of a manse for the church. After the sale of the former manse property at Pondfield Road and Midland Avenue, as already noted, the church for some years provided its minister with a rented home. After the selection of Dr. Ditzen as minister of the church, it was decided that the church should provide a dignified and attractive residence that would serve as a suitable and permanent manse. The substantial stone residence at 18 Masterton Road was thereupon purchased and was made available to Dr. Ditzen as a home for himself and his family when he came to Bronxville in September to assume his duties as minister of the church.

THE REV. LOWELL RUSSELL DITZEN, D.D.

THE Rev. Dr. Lowell Russell Ditzen was installed as the minister of the church at an impressive ceremony on Wednesday evening, October 4, 1950, in the presence of a large congregation.

Following the entrance of a notable group of distinguished clergymen, a Call to Worship was delivered by the presiding officer of the ceremony, the Rev. Arthur H. Voerman, president of the Classis of Westchester. After scripture reading, prayers and music, the sermon was preached by Dr. Henry P. Van Dusen, president of Union Theological Seminary. The Charge to the Minister was delivered by Dr. Paul Austin Wolfe, minister of the Brick Presbyterian Church of New York, and the Charge to the People by the Rev. Theodore H. Thielpape, minister of the Crescent Place Reformed Church of Yonkers, New York.

The declaration by the president of the Classis that Lowell Russell Ditzen was now duly installed as pastor of the Reformed Church of Bronxville was followed by a Prayer of Installation offered by the Rev. Deane Edwards, a former pastor of the church, and a benediction pronounced by Dr. Ditzen.

It was particularly gratifying that Dr. Ditzen had assumed leadership before the date of the one hundredth anniversary of the church, November 5, 1950.

The entire month of November was devoted to the celebration, which was planned by a special committee whose names may be found in the Appendix.

63

The month was marked by a series of special Sunday morning sermons by Dr. Ditzen, and mid-week organ recitals.

The topics of the four anniversary sermons were, "Highlights of Our Heritage," "This Nation Under God," "Into All the World" and "The Future Beckons."

The centennial celebration ended with a New Year's Day Tea, given in the assembly room of the church school, attended by some eighteen hundred happy parishioners, who came to rejoice over the anniversary, but more especially to honor Dr. and Mrs. Ditzen.

In connection with the centennial celebration, the *Book of Remembrance* was compiled under the direction of a committee composed of Arthur F. Corwin, chairman, and O. Dickinson Street and Harry Leslie Walker.

This handsomely printed and bound volume contains a permanent record of all the memorials which have been given to the church since its establishment. All are described in detail, and in each case there is given the name or names of the donors and of the individuals in whose honor the memorial was presented.

The text of the *Book of Remembrance* is similar to that of Chapter X of this volume, together with parts 14, 15, 16 and 17 of the Appendix.

Space is provided in the book for the description of future memorials.

In years to come, the *Book of Remembrance* will doubtless be one of the carefully cherished records of the church.

On November 1, 1950 the Rev. Ronald William Mc-
Neur became part-time assistant minister, working
especially with the young people, and entering as
much as possible into participation in all church activities. In December, announcement was made that
the University of Edinburgh, Scotland, had granted
him the degree of Doctor of Philosophy, upon the ac-
ceptance of the work he had completed before coming
to America. Announcement was also made that beginning May 1, 1951 Dr. McNeur would become full-time
resident assistant minister.

SEAL OF THE CLASSIS OF AMSTERDAM

65

And I saw a new heaven and a new earth: . . . And I heard a great voice out of heaven saying, Behold, the tabernacle of God is with men, and he will dwell with them, and they shall be his people, and God himself shall be with them, and be their God. . . . And he that sat upon the throne said, Behold, I make all things new. . . . REVELATION 21:1,3,5

CHAPTER IV

———◆———

THE FUTURE

By Dr. Lowell Russell Ditzen

TWO ELEMENTS should give us pause as we consider the future of our church.

For one thing, we may be sure that this church will have a tomorrow. It will live on, long past our physical life. The longing in the heart of man to worship his God and to achieve a victory in the living of life, that longing which brought this church into being, and which has nurtured it across the years, will be with the men and women of tomorrow. There will be a future for this church, as there is a past and as there is a today.

Then there is the sobering fact that our own plans, decisions, and actions now will have a determinative influence on that future. What is the "present" for us becomes the "heritage" of those yet unborn. The foundations we lay will be builded on a hundred years from now. It is pertinent then to consider what we do, not alone for its bearing on our own generation, but for the repercussions that will be forthcoming on the future. How imperative to build soundly!

Some years ago I read a letter written by a clergyman seventy-five years earlier to the unknown man who would be his successor in the pulpit. The document, just unsealed, was a tragedy. It viewed the present incumbent as living in a world of international peace. Churches were seen as being no longer divided. The light of God's Kingdom shown on endless communities where love was the only law and universal prosperity was the only rule.

I dare not engage in such uncertain prophecy. Yet of some things, may we not have surety as we consider the future of this church? My heart leads me to feel that the men and women of tomorrow will seek to live a goodly life. They will fail and falter, as do we. They will know sorrow and pain. They will love and laugh. But they will know what it is to weep inwardly while continuing the inexorable duties of the day. They will need faith and hope and camaraderie and comfort and peace. They will need God and the Church of Jesus Christ.

Though it seems inadvisable to conjecture as to what we will be in the future, it is important to state, as specifically as possible, the directions in which we ought to go.

To build soundly, is it not essential that the church keep to its central mission today and tomorrow, to let Jesus live; to make audible and delicate music from the world of the Spirit; to bring to men and women the Eternal Word of their God? Let us remind ourselves now that that is our primary task. That will mean that prayerful and continuous attention should be given to the worship of this church. The music, the readings, the prayers, the sermons should be an expression of the best possible gifts from those who accept responsibility in the ministries of word and song.

That high spirit of integrity and preparation, manifest on Sunday morning, must have a counterpart in the activity and programs throughout the week.

Particularly we must be attentive to our boys and girls and young people. It cannot be stated too often that what we do for them will determine the kind of church we have in the future. At the present time great care is being given to planning the strongest possible emphasis for the youth of the church. Beginning with birth, the Sacrament of Baptism will be made a simple but deeply significant experience. Help will be given, wherever needed, to parents of infants. Classes for tiny tots will be held during the church services so that the parents may participate in the worship. A nursery school for children, between the ages of three to five, will provide a program each morning during the week for small children to be under the influence of the church as they come together for play, music, and happy forms of group activity. The Church School and

68

the released time program during the week must offer the best possible instruction in a constructive and congenial atmosphere with the highest type leadership. Through high school, college, and post-college ages, organized activities must be a part of our church life to provide study, fellowship, service opportunities for the maturing life of our youth. At the time of marriage there will be counseling and guidance.

With love and intelligence we can impart to our children the best in our heritage. If we will dedicate ourselves to this mission, we may have the confidence that we are setting into motion the strongest possible forces to build the greater church of the future.

Again we cannot neglect the family as a unit. Our day particularly sees the family subject to innumerable pulls and claims. If, as in generations past, we can make the church "the meeting house," where families may come together for joy and instruction and fellowship, ours will be a good ministry today contributing to a more hopeful future.

Then there must be great tenderness and affectionate concern manifest by the church to the aged and the invalided. The care that is inspired by the compassion of Jesus will surely be manifest to all who are ill, who are lonely, who stand in the sunset days of life.

The program for mature men and women must ever be encouraged. There are tremendous resources in the intelligence and culture of our people. The capacities for powerful leadership in the New York area, throughout the nation, and the world are legion. To bring our men and women together in various societies and causes, to join hands and resources in meeting the opportunities of our day, is a task that the church must not neglect. Christian principles need applying in the complex social and economic and political relationships of our time. The men and women of this parish can make potent contributions in this area. To do it, however, their resources must be unified, challenged, channeled, and directed.

Once again the ministers must be available for individual counseling and help. Our heritage as Christians is one that has faith in the ministry of healing of body and mind and spirit. The field of psychosomatic medicine has verified in our modern times what the church has always known, that bedeviling problems and ills of the mind and heart can affect our outlooks and our physical states. To be of practical help to people who live in this present world, the resources of faith and of the wisdom as to how to live must be brought to bear in individual lives that are seeking and needing.

Then too, with the resources within our membership, we have opportunity to assume a moral and benevolent leadership for this whole metropolitan area. On moral questions that affect the total life of millions of people we must speak with clarity and act with courage. Living in the lovely and sequestered community of Bronxville we must prod ourselves from the temptation to "be at ease in Zion." The needs of the underprivileged, the dispossessed, the impoverished of the New York area must come to us and we must respond.

To develop such a strong and responsive church certain things are essential. We will need a strong staff, and we will need adequate space, equipment and facilities. At the present time the church is blessed with capable leadership, and an able committee is giving thought to our very apparent needs for added space and increased facilities.

When the present church was built our membership numbered six hundred souls. Today, the membership is more than three times that number. Increased activities and programs for men and women, boys and girls, require that we give thought and make serious effort at this time to improve and develop our physical resources for an effective ministry to our congregation and to the community.

The basic assumption of the above is that we minister most effectively to the future by doing the best possible job in our own time. In the spirit of the Master, we are dedicated to the extension of His spirit and His way in individual lives and in the corporate life of our community and nation.

We have a great and goodly spirit of expectancy and confidence with which to go forward toward the future. Let our spoken and unspoken petition simply be that "God leading us to do our best in the present, we would humbly strive to create a goodly heritage out of our today to bequeath to tomorrow."

With such a spirit inspiring our labors shall we not derive a blessing? And shall not those of tomorrow be blessed by our today?

71

THE KINDERGARTEN WINDOW

CHAPTER V

THE CHURCH SCHOOL

WHEN the early Dutch settlements were made in America, one of the required conditions was that "The City of Amsterdam shall send thither a proper person for school master, who shall also read the Holy Scriptures in public, and set the Psalms." This requirement was met when the first schoolmaster, Adam Roelandsen came in 1633. However, it is probable that the church schools were in operation as early as 1626, and were conducted by the "comforters of the sick" who preceded the arrival of the ministers and the school masters.

The second schoolmaster was Jan Cornelissen, whose term of office was from about 1635 to 1650. These men and all teachers were licensed to instruct by the civil and ecclesiastical authorities of Holland. Governor Stuyvesant at one time wrote to the Classis of Amsterdam to send "a pious, well qualified and diligent school master." "Nothing," he adds "is of greater importance than the right, early instruction of youth."

Wherever churches were organized they were followed by a school. Thus, in 1850, when the Bronxville church was organized, the first thought was for a school for the religious education of the young. Immediately therefore, a Church School was organized with an elder, James Minot Prescott, as the first superintendent. Classes for the older people also were held in the church and in private homes. The diary of Mrs. David E. Smith,

73

wife of the community physician, mentions a kindergarten class held in her husband's home office.

Mr. Prescott held the office of superintendent until 1874 when Alexander Masterton, Jr., assumed the leadership of the Church School and for twenty-five years gave it devoted and efficient service.

During these years the Church School grew to such an extent that an addition to the little church was considered a necessity. Mr. Masterton generously provided an assembly room as an addition. This furnished suitable quarters, as well, for social activities and young people's meetings. Mr. Masterton also started the first library for the teachers and students in the Church School. His grandson, Alex Ferris, son of Mr. and Mrs. William Nelson Ferris, was the first librarian.

It is interesting to note that in the original Church School roll book of May, 1862, two "contrabands," Stephen and Frank, were listed as members. These two colored boys were proteges of Mr. Swain who, during the Civil War, maintained a station of the "underground railroad" in his home.

Upon the death of Mr. Masterton in the year 1899, Frank R. Chambers, who had recently moved to Bronxville, became superintendent of the Church School. For twenty-two years Mr. Chambers went his kindly and inspiring way in the village and the church; and when in 1920, on account of failing health he gave up the active superintendency of the Church School, he continued to teach wherever he was needed, as superintendent emeritus until the fall of 1939. From 1919 to

1921, LaMont A. Warner was assistant superintendent of the Church School.

When Mr. Chambers decided to retire as active superintendent in 1920, he invited Prof. James Coffin Stout to become the leader of what was then known as the senior department. In the meantime, in January, 1919, Mrs. Otto J. Gette had become superintendent of the primary department, which position she still holds.

Prof. Stout was head of the Department of Church History at the Biblical Seminary in New York and brought to the school a background of rich experience. For seven years, teachers and students alike profited by his sound scholarship and Christian idealism.

When the Rev. Deane Edwards was installed as minister of the church in January, 1920, there was an enrollment of 460 pupils and 45 officers, teachers and assistants.

In 1928, Frederick L. Fay came to join the staff as Director of Religious Education and the students were separated into graded departments in order more adequately to meet their changing interests and spiritual needs.

For seven years Edward A. Yungel served as secretary of the senior department and after his death the lectern, which is still used every Sunday morning in the assembly room, was given in his memory by Mrs. Yungel.

Twenty-five or more years of untiring service were given by J. E. S. Barker to the Church School as teacher and secretary. When he retired to work with the choir and orchestra, several young people took turns at the secretary's desk.

A number of workers in the school in 1928 were still in active service in 1950: Mrs. Harry E. Warren, Mrs. B. K. Parker, Mrs. Gette, Miss Amie S. Dusenberry and Vernon T. Sanders. It was long before 1928, that Miss Dusenberry had organized the class of young men known as "The Board of Directors." During forty years, some nine hundred young men have been benefited by her guidance. Today, in every state of the Union, one or more affirm their devotion and loyalty to "Miss Amie."

Mr. Fay met with the Juniors for mission study, and on Sunday evenings led the Young People's Society in discussion and worship. After five years, he resigned leaving an active church school of about 550 pupils.

In 1930, when Dr. Powell became minister of the church, several changes occurred in the church school leadership. Miss Louise Weldon's place as head of the junior department was taken by Miss Ruth Scotford in 1937-38 and then by Miss Elizabeth Edland who resigned in 1941. Mrs. Daniel L. Grant then took charge of the department.

In July, 1933 the Rev. William McCance became Assistant Minister and Director of Religious Education. After five years, he too resigned to accept a call to the ministry of the Congregational Church at Middlebury, Connecticut.

The Rev. Howard C. Shaffer succeeded Mr. McCance in September, 1938. In 1940 he married Miss Elinor

Best, of Bronxville, and together they gave the young people an inspired leadership. In 1942 Mr. Shaffer resigned to become minister of the Colonial Church at Bayside, N. Y., and in October of that year Mrs. Gette became Director of Religious Education. Also in 1942, the Rev. Carl V. Herron, who had been teaching in the high school department since 1938, became superintendent of that department and has ever since given it the benefit of his rich and full experience.

In 1943 Mrs. Grant resigned from the junior department and Mrs. L. S. Albright assumed leadership. At this time, the pulpit that had formerly been used in the little old church replaced the table which Mrs. Grant had arranged as the worship center for the junior department. This department under Mrs. Albright's exceptional leadership had spread into every available corner of the building. When she moved away from Bronxville in November, 1948 the department was placed in the competent hands of Mrs. Hilda White, who had been an assistant to Mrs. Albright since 1944.

A great step forward was taken when on October 30, 1945, the school received a gift of a projector and screen from Arad Riggs, chairman of the religious education committee of Consistory, and John P. Holmes, a teacher in the senior department. Since that time there have been shown many pictures of inspirational as well as educational value.

In the Summer of 1945 the Rev. George Ackerly came to Bronxville as Associate Minister of the church. He taught in the Church School and supervised the showing of films, but his chief interest was in the Young People's Society and the Young Adult Group. In 1950, Mr. Ackerly resigned and became an assistant minister at the Church of the Covenant at Cleveland, Ohio.

The Church School sustained a great loss by the sudden death of Mrs. Pearle Boyd Bascom in December, 1947, after twenty years of consecrated and devoted service as superintendent of the kindergarten. Mrs. Paul Gregory took her place in January, 1948 and was followed the next year by Mrs. Lawrence Drake.

On February 5, 1950 the Church School opened its doors to a new group — a special class for handicapped children regardless of age, race or color. Miss Marie Desborough became the first teacher. It was a thrilling adventure to lead these children into their first group experience. So far as is known, this is the first class of its kind in the country. Public-spirited men of the community built special chairs and tables needed by the children. A group of ninth grade Church School girls with their teacher, Mrs. Albert E. Morgan, have published a paper called "The Little Light," for the enjoyment of these children and their parents. It is to be used also as a means of carrying news of the project to interested leaders elsewhere.

The Sunday offerings of the Church School are devoted entirely to benevolences. This is considered a part of the school's task in educating the students in intelligent giving.

As a part of its educational program, the Church School conducts week day classes during released time from the Bronxville Public School and Yonkers School No. 8. In 1950 approximately one hundred pupils took advantage of this opportunity for religious instruction under competent leadership.

The enrollment for 1949-1950 listed 576 pupils, 49 officers and teachers and 105 cradle roll children under three years of age.

"AS A LILY AMONG THORNS"

*She seeketh wool, and flax,
and worketh willingly with her hands.*

*She stretcheth out her hands to the poor;
yea, she reacheth forth her hands to the
     needy.*

*She openeth her mouth with wisdom;
and in her tongue is the law of kindness.*
                    PROVERBS 31:13,20,26

CHAPTER VI

THE WOMEN'S SOCIETY

THE first record we have of any kind of woman's organization in the Bronxville Church was in the early 1860's during the Rev. Washington Roosevelt's ministry. These Civil War days were exciting times, and women as well as men were apprehensive. In 1851 Harriet Beecher Stowe published *Uncle Tom's Cabin* in serial form and in 1852 in book form. The whole country was stirred by this as well as by several other books from her pen.

By the time the war actually began, the women of the community had formed the "Ladies' Sewing Society of the Reformed Church of Bronxville." The object of the society was to aid the church and further its interests in whatever way might be desirable. Meetings were held twice a month, when shirts and havelocks were made for the soldiers. Mrs. William Nelson Ferris relates that all the women assembled at the church to "pick lint" and make bandages for the wounded. The men were invited to attend these meetings at supper time. Mr. Roosevelt came in his buggy from his home in Pelham, never missing a meeting unless he was ill. His means of transportation had been provided by the sewing society which gave a supper in Temperance Hall, Tuckahoe, to raise money to buy a horse and buggy for Mr. Roosevelt.

The Ladies' Sewing Society must have been an enterprising group. A fair was held in the Yonkers Armory and many other entertainments were given for the benefit of the soldiers. On January 10, 1858 the "Lady Sewers" by unanimous vote turned over to the church treasurer, Mr. Masterton, the sum of $100 to help pay church expenses. Later, this society was merged with the present Women's Society.

At the call of the new minister, the Rev. A. E. Myers, nine ladies gathered in January, 1874 at the chapel, as the small colonial church was often called. The purpose was to organize the group for Christian work and education beyond the somewhat narrow limits of purely local interest.

This new organization was "an auxiliary to the Women's Foreign Missionary Society of the Reformed Church in America" and was called "The Bronxville Auxiliary." A constitution and by-laws were adopted, stating that the object of the society was "to aid the General Society in sending out and maintaining female missionaries, Bible readers and teachers who shall work among heathen women and children."

The nine ladies on that memorable occasion were: Mrs. A. E. Myers, wife of the pastor; Mrs. David E. Smith, who was the former Miss Araminta Swain; Mrs. Swain, Mrs. Prescott, Mrs. Underhill, Mrs. S. H. Cox, Miss Latimer, Miss Lyman and Miss Jeanette Chambers. Miss Lyman was elected president and held that office for many years; Mrs. Alexander Masterton, vice-president; Mrs. Francis Bacon, secretary; and Mrs. A. G. Burtnett, treasurer.

At the second meeting of the newly formed "Auxiliary," twenty ladies were present. Letters were read from the Rev. J. M. Ferris, corresponding secretary of the Foreign Missions Board, and from Mrs. Miller, a teacher in the Girls' School at Yokohama, Japan, describing the school. At a meeting a few months later, it was resolved to send financial aid to the school, in the form of a scholarship of $60 which was enough to pay for tuition, board and necessary clothing for a student for a year. This school was known later as Ferris Seminary. The ladies of the auxiliary also became interested in a school in Calcutta, India, and engaged a speaker to lecture to them about it.

During this first year of existence, the auxiliary had very meager resources. Attendance at meetings averaged about twelve, and members' dues of one dollar per year did not go very far. However, eight of the younger women were designated "collectors," and were required to call on each of the forty-six families in the vicinity. In this way, total receipts of $115 were raised, much of which was used to pay for the expenses and time of the lecturers. However, the ladies were sufficiently encouraged to decide to continue the society for another year. Little did they imagine that the interest they aroused would continue from that day to the present.

It must be admitted that there were times when a year or two would elapse without meetings, when the church lacked a full-time minister, or when the ladies' hands were too busy at home to spare time to devote to the work of the organization. Sometimes, even in active years, the minutes record that there had been no meeting during a certain month because of bad weather. A vision of the ladies walking through mud, snow or dust, sometimes for long distances, or driving to the meeting place in a carriage makes one realize the sacrifices necessary to carry on the work.

Once or twice during those early years financial crises that were a part of the nation's history were felt in the Women's Foreign Missionary Society, too. Dues were reduced to two cents a meeting and the ladies were greatly concerned to help the mother society which had incurred indebtedness to meet its obligations in order that the mission schools could be continued. The "Star of Hope Mission Band," the young girls' society, helped in this and other emergencies. Organized in 1876, the girls had virtually the same interests as their elders. All together, young and old, held fancy work and cake sales and worked together to raise money.

A few years later, in 1880, there was a reorganization which brought the work of the Home Missions into the program. The society was now called the Women's Union Missionary Society. Interest in the work of missionaries abroad was supplemented by such activities as sending barrels of new clothing and children's toys and books to home missionaries in Kentucky and Indiana and among the American Indians. The society also helped to furnish church parsonages, and supplied communion services for western churches which were just getting started.

At the November meeting in 1881, it was resolved that the "Ladies' Sewing Society" have weekly meetings and become a part of the Union Missionary Society. This was the origin of the sewing committee of the present Women's Society, which in 1950 completed 959 articles of clothing and 3,350 surgical dressings.

For some time the growth of the Missionary Society was slow. For several years the average attendance at meetings was five. The amount of money collected was small. In 1892-1893, the total receipts were "Home Missions $10, Foreign Missions $10.02, total $20.02." Many of the annual reports were written by Miss Rosalie Bacon who alternated with her sister, Miss Anna Bacon as secretary of the society for many years. Their sister-in-law, Mrs. William P. H. Bacon is still an active member of the society. These ladies were daughters and daughter-in-law of Mrs. Francis Bacon, one of the founders of the society.

The annual reports are full of color. In one, Miss Bacon wrote, "We have a very discouraging report, but we are not dead yet." And again, "The ladies, feeling the need of more interest in missions and desiring to be more imbued with the spirit of the Master, spent a short time in earnest prayers for God's blessing on us as a society and as a church."

Miss Agnes Dusenberry and later her sister, Miss Amie S. Dusenberry, took a prominent part in the development of the society, Miss Agnes being one of the collectors appointed during the early years of its existence. She continued throughout a long life to be a leader in the devotional and spiritual life of the society.

As time went on, the prayers of the good ladies were answered. With the increasing population of Bronxville, and greater efforts on the part of the officers and members of the society, interest grew and membership increased. For two successive years, a bazaar was held at the Lawrence Park Casino which brought in more than $100 each time. Some of the money was used for local needs, some given to New York City work among sailors and others, and annual donations were increased to both Mission Boards.

In June of 1904, Mrs. Robertson, wife of the minister, organized a new society called the Church Aid Society. Its object was "to promote the interests of the Reformed Church in Bronxville and to do mission work in the community and throughout the world."

Under the chairmanship of various vice-presidents, a boys' club was started and a young women's and a children's club, along with the usual sewing, social and missionary committees. The young women's club, called the Earnest Workers' Circle of the King's Daughters was the nucleus of the present-day, local branch of that world-wide organization, while the little girls' club, the Whatsoever Society grew into today's League for Service.

Original members of the Church Aid Society numbered twenty-two and dues were twenty-five cents per year. Of the twenty-two members, several are still actively interested in the present Women's Society. Money was raised for church equipment including greatly needed new kitchen furnishings, and a sizable fund was contributed towards the church organ. In 1910, the Lawrence Hospital then in its first year was given ten dollars.

During this time, the Women's Missionary Auxiliary, the Church Aid Society and the Summer Sewing Guild were actively engaged in their separate activities. They had been founded many years before and were continuing along independent but over-lapping lines. Many women were members of all three groups.

After due consideration and the formulation of a workable plan, a joint meeting of the Missionary Auxiliary and the Church Aid Society was held on April 3, 1912. A resolution uniting the two groups was unanimously approved, and proper amendments to the constitution were adopted to implement this action. (The King's Daughters, Whatsoever Society and Crusaders, the boys' club, not being integral parts of the Reformed Church were omitted from the consolidation and carried on by themselves).

86

Thus was the present Women's Society originated. Mrs. Barrett Andrews (the present Mrs. William L. Colt) and Mrs. Harry Leslie Walker were the guiding spirits in this organization. Mrs. Andrews was elected the first president and Mrs. Walker the recording secretary, and they are both still actively interested in the society. Many of the provisions of the constitution and by-laws adopted in 1912 are to be found in the new constitution and by-laws prepared by a committee under the chairmanship of Mrs. Walker and adopted in 1950.

The union of the societies accomplished what was hoped for: more interest, more members, a greater knowledge of the work of the church and a new enthusiasm for its accomplishment, and increased spiritual growth for the individual members.

Regular all-day monthly meetings are held on the second Wednesday of each month from September (when for that one month only it is held on the third Wednesday) through June. Beginning at 9:45, sewing and the preparation of surgical dressings occupy the members. At 11:30 occurs a worship service, followed by a short business meeting and an address. In December, 1950 Dr. Harry Emerson Fosdick, a fellow-townsman, was the speaker, his subject being "A Christmas Message." Luncheon is served at 1:00, after which work is resumed on sewing and surgical dressings.

During the Lenten season, meetings are held every Wednesday when hospital supplies are prepared for the mission hospitals in Kuwait, Arabia.

When the need for help in many activities became apparent at the time of World War I, the 155 members of the society added Red Cross work and emergency nursing during the influenza epidemic to their usual work. They volunteered their services in many special activities necessitated by war conditions. In 1918, monthly afternoon meetings were held mid-way between the regular all-day ones.

At about this time, religious services in Finnish were conducted under the auspices of the society and a club for Finnish women was sponsored. A weekly evening class to teach English to adults was organized and later transferred to the public school.

An increased interest in missions was fostered by visits to the Women's Society of a number of outstanding people who were in this country on furlough from the mission fields. Among them were Mrs. Sharon J. Thoms of Basrah, Mrs. Stanley Mylrea of Kuwait and Dr. Paul Harrison who had traveled widely in Arabia, and was the only white man to have penetrated parts of that country; Miss Edna Beekman of Amoy, China; and the beloved and distinguished Dr. Ida Scudder of India.

In 1924, a milestone was reached and the society celebrated its Golden Jubilee, the fiftieth year after its original organization. The meeting was a large one, and was held in the main body of the church — still the little white colonial church — instead of in the church parlor and Sunday School room, as was customary. Into the front pews, to the tune of "Onward Christian

Soldiers," marched early dignitaries of the society, past presidents, and devoted members of the earlier organizations. It was an inspiring occasion, and one that developed interest and enthusiasm.

Late in 1926, the new church was finished and the transition from the small white one was completed. For three years or more, the Women's Society added special activities to its regular program and raised the sum of $6,152 towards the cost of the new church.

Monthly afternoon meetings with the women of the West Center Church were started in January, 1923 and continued for many years. The program was much like that of the main society — sewing, devotions and an address.

Joint study of missions with women of Christ Church began in January, 1922 and continued for several years, with meetings held three or four times a year.

The Annual Union Meeting of the women of five of the Bronxville churches has become a village tradition. In October, 1926 a joint rally was organized by the women of Christ Church (Episcopal) and those of the Reformed Church. In 1930 the West Center Church Society (Congregational) and St. Joseph's Society (Roman Catholic) joined the group. In 1942 the Concordia Women's Guild (Lutheran) also joined. In addition to hearing a distinguished speaker, the women sew and make surgical dressings for Lawrence Hospital, Grasslands Hospital, Rosary Hill Cancer Hospital and for Yonkers' Family Service. Fellowship is promoted during the luncheon hour. The offering taken at the service is distributed among causes in which all the participating organizations are interested.

The idea of the Annual Union meetings was originated by Mrs. Deane Edwards, wife of the minister of the Reformed Church at that time. Mrs. Edwards, a sister of John Foster Dulles, is an outstanding authority in the field of religious education, and is the author of a number of important books upon the subject.

The Union meetings are held the second Wednesday in November, the place of meeting being by rotation. In November, 1950 it was held in the Reformed Church, when the speaker was Mrs. Douglas Horton.

The Women's Society numbered four hundred members by March, 1931 and easily met an annual budget of $6,000. There was keen interest in missions, both foreign and domestic, with the society's funds being sent directly to specific causes rather than to the Women's Board of Foreign and Domestic Missions. Mission study classes were well attended, and projects in Tuckahoe, in New York and at the Children's Village at Dobbs Ferry were added to the obligations of the society. At the time of the general business depression, the budget was reduced to $5,000, but was again gradually increased to $6,000.

The year 1940 brought the distant rumblings of war in Europe. Again, as before, the members rose to meet new demands. Courses taught by the Red Cross in home nursing, first aid, hospital nurses' aid and nutrition were well attended. Production of surgical dressings, and garments sewed and knitted under Red Cross guidance were added to the regular activities of the members.

As the war continued, it was learned that several of the foreign missionaries were under fire. News was eagerly and anxiously awaited. It was a great relief when assurance came that none had been injured.

At the September meeting of 1945, the women of the society joined in heartfelt prayers of thanksgiving for the end of World War II, which had occurred the previous month. At the same time there was emphasized the importance of turning the time and energy formerly devoted to the war effort, into the problems of reconstruction and the firm establishment of peace.

In April of the centennial year, 1950, the Society numbered 471. Average attendance at meetings was 185. The benevolence budget was $6,000 and dues of $5 per year paid for the running expenses and for the luncheons served at each of nine all-day monthly meetings, where there is no individual luncheon fee. The luncheon committee served, during the year, 1,638 luncheons at a cost of 32 cents each.

There were twenty-one standing committees, some of which conducted the affairs of the society, and some had oversight of the church building and grounds. The Missionary Committee kept the members informed in many interesting ways about foreign and domestic missions. The Sewing Committee made garments, layettes and surgical dressings for local and foreign projects in Yonkers and Tuckahoe, Kentucky, India and Arabia.

91

The Membership Committee called upon members of the church as well as of the society and served a delightful tea, an annual fall event, for the membership.

In 1949 a new group was formed, composed of those women who wished to participate in the work and fellowship of the society, but who were unable to attend regular meetings because of business or professional duties. These women meet in the evening, call themselves the Evening Group, and have a pleasant and interesting time together. They have given material aid to many worthy objects.

Each year, a delegate from the Women's Society is sent to the Northfield Missionary Conference at Northfield, Massachusetts. The reports brought back to the society by the delegates are inspirational as well as informative, and stimulate the members to more effective participation in the world's work.

The executive board of the society meets regularly, once a month, under the leadership of the president. At these meetings, reports on current work are heard and discussed, plans are made for future activities, and the allocation of funds is considered and determined. For the term of office up to and including the time of the centennial, the president was Mrs. Francis B. Whitlock. The recently elected president is Mrs. Jackson Chambers.

CHAPTER VII

THE MEN'S CLUB

THE first mention of an organization of men to assist in the work of the church, appears late in the pastorate of Dr. Robertson. At a meeting of Consistory on May 15, 1912, the idea of a men's organization was suggested and the matter was referred to the minister and elders. At a special meeting of Consistory held one week later, the subject was discussed and action was taken to the effect that "in the main the suggestion had the approval of the Pastor and Elders."

If such an association was formed, there is no record of its activities, and the idea of an active men's organization seems to have remained dormant until early in the pastorate of Mr. Edwards.

In the year 1922, pursuant to action of Consistory at its meeting of April 8th, Mr. Edwards met with two of his deacons, F. Bradley Reynolds and Thomas B. Gilchrist, at the home of Rolland J. Hamilton (who became a deacon the following year), to discuss the formation of a men's association. As a result of this discussion, the Men's Club was organized and Mr. Hamilton was chosen as the first president. The first meeting was held December 7, 1922.

For several years the club held monthly meetings except during the summer months. The meetings were largely social in character, and it was customary to have an address at each one by some well-known person, on a subject of interest to the members of the organization. Topics of local, national or international consequence, as well as those of a charitable or eleemosynary nature were discussed. Light refreshments were served at the close of the meeting. At the final meeting held in the spring of each year, an outstanding speaker was secured whose subject would be of general interest, when the women of the congregation were invited to be present and to enjoy the hospitality of the club.

An attempt was made to foster some particular worthy object in order that the club might not exist as simply a social organization. However, the difficulty of obtaining speakers of note, and the failure to identify the club with an enterprise of sufficient importance to develop concern on the part of the members resulted in

94

a decline in interest. Finally, the club stopped holding regular meetings, and became practically dormant.

It was in the fall of 1939 that Dr. Powell, with the aid of two former presidents of the club, Clinton C. Swan and George F. Parton, brought about a revival of interest in the Men's Club. It was reorganized, and membership was made available to all men of the community without restriction as to denomination or church affiliation. The dues were fixed at one dollar per year. Instead of occurring on a regular, stated evening of each month, meetings were held subject to the call of the president. They took place, then, only at such times as outstanding speakers were available to address the club.

The new club attained vigor and developed enthusiastic interest among the men of the church and community, due largely to the cooperation of Clarence Francis, a member of the Reformed Church. Being president and later chairman of the board of General Foods Corporation and having a wide acquaintance among men prominent in the affairs of the nation, Mr. Francis aided the officers of the club by bringing distinguished speakers to Bronxville on various occasions to address the club.

Other club members also obtained prominent men as speakers, who were available because of friendship.

Some of those who addressed the club were: Herbert Hoover, Lewis Douglas, Edward R. Stettinius, W. Averell Harriman, William S. Knudsen, Arthur Capper, Eric A. Johnston, Paul Hoffman, Alfred P. Sloan,

Jr., Henry Ford II, Philip D. Reed, and "Eddie" Rickenbacker.

During the decade following its reorganization in 1939, the Men's Club filled to capacity the assembly room of the church where the meetings were held. Attendance on occasion numbered as high as five hundred individuals and it was often necessary, due to lack of space, to turn away many who sought admittance.

The interest of the club was maintained not alone by the privilege of listening to outstanding speakers. Worthy charitable projects were sponsored by the club. This stimulated in the minds of the members a desire to be of service and did, indeed, elevate the purpose of the club above that of a purely social organization.

Funds were raised to equip and send a field kitchen to Norway for use in World War II, in acknowledgment of which the club received a gracious letter of thanks from His Majesty, King Haakon VII.

Funds were also raised to equip a second field kitchen which was sent to the United States forces in Italy during World War II.

Of local interest was the financing of a scholarship at the Bronxville High School.

An unemployment committee headed by George F. Parton, the first president of the reorganized club, was instrumental in finding positions for many residents of Bronxville, both men and women, during the critical period of the early years of World War II. This committee has continued its work as a clearing house for unemployed persons. It has been successful in obtaining satisfactory work for the unemployed, owing to the fact that the membership of the club includes many New York business executives, employers of labor, professional men and leaders in various fields of industry. Their cooperation is of great value.

The present president of the Men's Club is Paul E. Tobin.

PULPIT IN THE OLD CHURCH

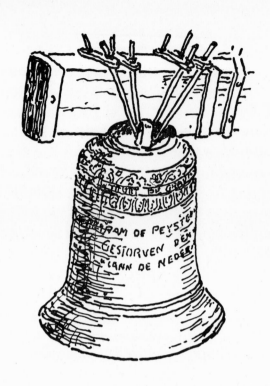

CHAPTER VIII

THE MUSIC

IN the early days of the colony of New Amsterdam and before the arrival of the first minister, two men, Bastiaen Jansen Kroll and Jan Huyck, known as Kranken-bezoekers or comforters of the sick, had "read to the commonalty on Sundays texts of Scripture and the creeds and set the Psalms." These were the song leaders of the day. We find no record that any musical instrument was used until nearly a century later.

It is believed that the first organ used in a church in New York was brought from Europe by Governor

William Burnet in 1720. In 1728 this instrument was given to the Old South Church in Garden Street, New York, where it was used until Revolutionary times. After the devastations of the British occupation during the war, the organ was not to be found. It was probably taken to England. ·

The tuning fork was used in the Bronxville Church until late in the 1860's. Mr. Prescott, one of the elders, was strongly opposed to the introduction of "mechanical" music in the service, deeming it "Popery and the work of the Devil." About 1870, however, during the Rev. Washington Roosevelt's ministry, Mr. Masterton, disregarding Mr. Prescott's strenuous objections, presented a Mason and Hamlin reed organ to the church. It was installed in the gallery at the rear of the church. Mr. Masterton's daughter Louise (later Mrs. William Nelson Ferris) was appointed organist. She was then about sixteen years old. Mrs. Ferris is now ninety-eight years of age, the church's oldest living member. All of her long, busy life she has been an active church member, deeply interested in all its work and greatly beloved by all who know her.

At the time when the organ was installed, a choir was organized and led by Dr. David E. Smith, son-in-law of James P. Swain. Mrs. Crocker was the second organist and was followed by Miss Araminta Smith who later became Mrs. Harry Schenck. The small reed organ was in due time replaced by a vocalion.

In 1906 the church was renovated and the gallery removed. Then, in an alcove built for it, a small pipe organ was installed. This was a good instrument and was in use until the new church was built.

During the ministry of Mr. Runk, Miss Rosalie Bacon, daughter of Francis Bacon, became the organist in 1882, and held that position for twenty-five years. By this time the music of the church had become an important part of the service.

In 1902, Mrs. Frank E. Kavanagh was engaged as the soloist, and for twenty years was an active member of the choir.

Following Miss Bacon, Mrs. Walden Lasky was organist and choir director. During Dr. Robertson's ministry she organized and trained a vested choir of young people.

Miss Winnifred Rohrer was the next organist and it was during this time that Graham MacNamee, who afterwards achieved fame as a radio sports announcer, sang for nine years as baritone and precentor.

The next leader was Blanche DaCosta Whitney, a soprano singer, who for some time was soloist and choir leader. Working with her were Marguerite Clark, contralto; George Reinhardt, tenor; Jackson Kinsey, bass; and Mildred Miles, organist.

On the evening of November 19, 1925, during the Rev. Deane Edwards' ministry, a group of musically inclined people met at the parsonage to form a choir which might sing at the community services held on Sunday evenings in the old church. The newly organized choir, consisting of ten members, sang at its first Sunday evening service on December 6, 1925. Jackson

Kinsey was director of this choir and Mildred Miles the organist, a combination of leadership which is still in effect. The choir continued to sing in the old church until April 4, 1926.

On that day, which was Easter Sunday, the choir sang in the new assembly hall which was completed and ready for services.

In May of that year Jackson Kinsey became the baritone soloist and director of the choir.

At the dedication service in the new church, December 19, 1926, a new large choir was assembled. There was a chorus of twenty voices and a quartette composed of the following: Hilda Jones, soprano; Elaine Horton-Mace, contralto; Richard Hunt, tenor; Jackson Kinsey, bass and director; and Mildred Miles, organist.

Warren Lee Terry replaced Mr. Hunt as tenor soloist on May 1, 1927. Harold Branch, tenor soloist and well known broadcaster over N.B.C., succeeded Mr. Terry on May 1, 1928; and on May 1, 1935, Eugene Mott became and still is tenor soloist.

During the past twenty-five years the church has had some prominent soloists from the Metropolitan Opera Company: tenors, Lambert Murphy and George Rasely; soprano, Jean Merrill; contraltos, Winifred Heidt and Lucille Cummings.

The present choir consists of thirty-two members and the quartette: Henrietta Green, soprano; Alice Tobin, contralto; Eugene Mott, tenor; Jackson Kinsey, bass and director; and Mildred Miles, organist.

101

Many outstanding musical services have been offered at the church. The first Oratorio was presented December 26, 1926. The choir then sang Handel's "Messiah." This selection has been repeated each Christmas season.

The church has a Junior Choir, under the direction of Eugene Mott, which is a part of the educational program of the Church School. This choir sings as a unit at the first service on Easter Sunday morning and on Children's Day.

The quartette and full choir sing special music at Christmas and Easter, and always a well-known cantata on the evening of Good Friday.

The pipe organ in the church is a fine instrument made and installed by Hook and Hastings. It has three manuals and a wide range of tone qualities. There are 2,446 pipes, and seven miles of wiring.

Two series of organ recitals have been presented during the last year.

Each Sunday morning the memorial chimes ring out their deep, sonorous tones, telling the Bronxville community that service is about to begin at the Reformed Church. They have been rung, for the most part, by the younger members of the congregation. The bell ringers have performed a great service for the church which is sincerely appreciated by the community.

When the bells cease ringing, Miss Miles renders an Organ Prelude.

The congregation stands when the vested choir is heard beginning the first hymn. The choir and the clergy advance into the church, the congregation joining in the processional hymn. When the choir stalls are filled and the hymn is ended, the minister pronounces the call to worship and offers an invocation, and all join in the Lord's Prayer.

Thus begins the morning worship service in the Bronxville Reformed Church.

THE ORGAN SCREEN

LOOKING OUT FROM THE CLOISTER GARDEN

104

CHAPTER IX

WORLDWIDE INTERESTS OF THE BRONXVILLE CHURCH

FROM the time of its origin, the Reformed Church of Bronxville has been a missionary-minded church. Not only has it contributed of its means to the Boards of the Reformed Church in America, but it has received constant inspiration by meeting with missionary leaders who became close personal friends of members of the church. They were stimulating guests, who came not merely to give an address but to remain sometimes for many days of rest, and friendly intercourse with groups both large and small. These visitors brought information, social, political and economic as well as religious, which enlarged the vision and strengthened the devotion of their hosts as well as of the entire membership of the church.

The Reformed Church in America has furnished great leaders in many fields throughout the world. Historically related to the founders of New Amsterdam, its especial province was to help to establish new churches for later immigrants from the Netherlands.

The first denomination to establish a theological seminary in this country was the Reformed Church in America. Established in 1784 in New Brunswick, New Jersey, adjoining the campus of Rutgers University, it is known as the New Brunswick Theological Seminary. The Bronxville church has been an annual contributor

to the seminary for many years, and has been represented by one of its elders on the Board of Trustees.

This church has always contributed also to a Ministers' Fund which provides relief and pensions to disabled and retired ministers and their widows. Within
the last few years, too, the church has contributed both
funds and talent to provide a home for aged ministers
and other full-time church workers. This opportunity
was made available by the gift to the Reformed Church
in America of "Kirkside," the former home of Helen
Gould Shepard in Roxbury, New York.

The American Bible Society, which circulates annually an average of eight million Bibles or Bible portions,
in 1,108 languages, receives regular contributions from
this church.

"Church World Service, Inc." was organized by the
merging of several relief organizations. Practically all
the churches in America united for the distribution of
their relief funds. The Bronxville Reformed Church
contributed a notable sum of money to this agency
which was under the executive direction of Dr. A. L.
Warnshuis.

The Federal Council of the Churches of Christ in
America has for some time received an annual contribution directly from the Bronxville Reformed Church.
Largely through the efforts of its general secretary for
the past thirty years, the Rev. Dr. Samuel McCrea
Cavert, a member of the Bronxville Reformed Church,
this organization has united with several others in
one organization called "The National Council of the

Churches of Christ in the United States of America." Its purpose is to correlate the work of American churches in all fields of service, and to develop practical programs of cooperation. Dr. Cavert continues as general secretary of the new organization, and the Rev. Deane Edwards as chairman of the Commission on Worship.

HOME MISSIONS

WHILE the interest of the Bronxville church in each of the above-mentioned enterprises is sincerely deep and generous, there are certain other projects within the borders of the United States in which the church and the Women's Society have assumed definite responsibility. These include work among the American Indians in the West, the Negroes in the South and in New York, the Mountaineers in Kentucky, and the Migrant Workers.

THE AMERICAN INDIANS

In Nebraska, Oklahoma and New Mexico, the Reformed Church workers among the American Indians have demonstrated in many ways that their fellow-Americans care for them and desire to help them socially, educationally and spiritually. Much progress has been made in freeing them from the terrors of old superstitions and health-wrecking habits. As is the policy in all Reformed Church work, the people of a locality contribute what they can towards church support, and they elect their own officers. At the request of government commissioners, through the Council of

Home Missions, the Bronxville Reformed Church missionaries to the Indians have given practical assistance in interpreting the changing policies of the Indian Commissioners.

THE NEGROES

In the southern states, among the Negroes, the Bronxville church has made its contribution through the Southern Normal School in Brewton, Alabama. In a wooded area of the state near the border of Florida, this Christian school has developed from humble beginnings into an outstanding institution. With 350 pupils in elementary and high schools, it has attained the highest rating for Negro schools in the state and the United States. The challenge of a school year of nine months with good buildings and good teachers, as contrasted with four-month sessions in neglected school houses with poorly educated teachers, has resulted in better schools and teachers throughout the county and surrounding area. In the county, 85% of the teachers are graduates of Brewton Southern Normal School. In 1950, Brewton had the third largest representation of Alabama cities at the State College at Montgomery. Although the first Brewton student was graduated from college as recently as 1939, there are now more than three hundred college graduates who are Brewton alumni. The principal, the Rev. Andrew Branche, is a graduate of the New Brunswick Theological Seminary. In 1950, the ministers of the city of Brewton accepted him as a member of their association. Mr. Branche and his wife, with their colleagues, have demonstrated to people in both northern and southern states that minds dedicated to Christian service can solve the most difficult problems. For some years the Bronxville Reformed Church has contributed scholarships, and the salaries of several faculty members to this excellent Normal School at Brewton.

In 1950 the church was represented by Miss Marie J. Lewis, Dean; and Mr. E. C. Hendrieth, Director of Farm Management.

In the city of New York, the condition in which the Negro and Porto Rican people live in Harlem, presents a real challenge to the church. Several denominations, including the Reformed Church in America are co-operating in a program for improvement of the social, recreational and spiritual life of this area. The women of the Bronxville church are deeply concerned and are sharing in this constructive effort to find the answer to this as yet unsolved problem.

THE MOUNTAINEERS

Just a half-century ago, in the foothills of south central Kentucky, the descendants of Scotch-Irish pioneers were living in unsanitary cabins on the poorest patches of farm land, in Jackson County. They had little or no access to church or school or medical aid, and but little to eat and wear. For months at a time, in Winter and Spring, the mountain foot paths and horse trails were impassable. It took the first missionaries a whole day in a jolting cart to go from Berea to McKee, a distance of forty miles. During fifty years of missionary service in Jackson County, however, the first small free day-school with four-month yearly sessions at McKee has developed into a fully accredited high school and boarding school at Annville. This institution, having a program of study combined with practical work, has taught 130 boys and girls each year to earn their tuition in part, and to fit themselves for Christian leadership in all fields of endeavor among their own people in the mountains and elsewhere. For some years the Women's Society of the Bronxville church has paid the salary of a much needed nurse in this district, the representative in 1950 being Miss Norine R. Swanson. Also, the society has provided scholarships for several pupils in the Annville school. No matter how poor these people may be, they wish to pay whatever they can towards their church and its services. At the "tradin' store" or thrift shop, they watch eagerly for the clothing and materials sent from the Bronxville and other Reformed churches.

THE MIGRANT WORKERS

The Migrant Workers, who, as the term signifies, lead a nomadic life, in following the seasons' planting and harvesting from place to place, are perhaps the most under-privileged of laborers. The recreational, medical and spiritual needs of this group have been met in a few camps, which are maintained by the employers. They call upon religious leaders who have had experience with professional and youth groups. The number of such workers, however, is entirely inadequate. Changing conditions, due to the mechanization of large farms and the freezing of produce, is bringing about a new situation, in that thousands of Porto Ricans, South Americans and Mexicans who formerly were seasonal workers or migrants, will become permanent settlers. This will pose a new problem and responsibility for the churches. The Women's Society of the Bronxville church has for many years given financial support to this worthy cause.

FOREIGN MISSIONS

THE missionary work of the Bronxville church in foreign countries is to be found for the most part in four countries, China, India, Arabia and Iraq, where the church and the Women's Society make substantial contributions directly to the projects they support.

Through its contributions to the Board of Foreign Missions, the church has had a considerable share also in educational missionary work in Japan. Two well-known schools for girls, Ferris Seminary in Yokohama and Sturgis Seminary in Shimonoseki have for many years enlisted the interest of members of the Women's Society. The Women's Christian University in Tokyo receives a part of the contributions offered when the women of all Bronxville Protestant churches meet in February for the Annual World Day of Prayer.

Another educational institution which receives support from the Bronxville church is the American University in Cairo, Egypt.

CHINA

The finest harbor and trading center on the southeast coast of China is Amoy. It is also a center of particular interest to the Bronxville church, because for many years the Women's Society has provided the basic salary of Miss Edna K. Beekman, the missionary teacher in the girls' elementary school in Amoy. Miss Beekman went to China in 1914, and she remained there even during the first years of World War II. She was repatriated on the "Gripsholm" in 1943. She returned to Amoy after the war and continued to be actively engaged in the school there, working as an advisor under the administration of Chinese principals. However, Miss Beekman has now been obliged to return again to America.

Miss Christina Holkeboer, to whose support while developing a girls' high school in Amoy the Women's Society also contributed, is now working among the Chinese on the islands of Indonesia.

Dr. A. L. Warnshuis spent many years in the missionary enterprise in China, and while there, published in 1911 his *Language Lessons in the Amoy Vernacular*. In addition to its great value in the Christian education of the Chinese people, this work became extremely important at the time of World War II, as an aid to intercourse between the Americans and the Chinese.

INDIA

The Bronxville Reformed Church has been fortunate in its relations with the missions in India. Dr. Ida Scudder, a granddaughter of the founder of the Arcot Mission, has enthused the members of the church during her many visits to it, when she described her hospital and road-side clinics. She established at Vellore in South India, the first medical school for women in India. Within recent years this school has been opened to men students. It is recognized by the Indian government as a part of the University of Madras, and it is now the only high grade missionary medical school in India. Some forty American, British and European missionary societies unite in its support.

With the exception of the relatively small, extremely wealthy class, the population of India lives chiefly in small villages and rural districts, and most of the people are illiterate and desperately poor.

Thirty years ago, a graduate of the Agricultural College of Iowa, John J. DeValois and his wife went to India as missionaries of the Reformed Church in America. Along with the Christian message, they wished to demonstrate to the people of India what they could do to help themselves by means of scientific methods of farming and the breeding of better animals and chickens as well as by using improved strains of vegetables, grains and fruit trees.

In 1922, Mr. DeValois acquired a barren waste of 175 acres, which he turned into a productive dry farm at Katpadi, six miles from Vellore. In 1944, with the help of the Bronxville Reformed Church he bought a well-watered farm of 132 acres nearby. In his agricultural Institute 114 boys are in training to become

113

Christian agricultural leaders. The graduates of this institute are in demand, everywhere.

To mention but one of his important projects, Mr. DeValois now has a five thousand egg incubator, the largest in India, and he has organized a cooperative egg marketing society with dependable standards of produce. As part of a government extension program, his goats and day-old chickens have been sent all over India and up the Burma Road. Those best qualified to judge recognize Mr. DeValois as one who is doing some of the most important and effective missionary work in India. The Bronxville Reformed Church has had the privilege of providing the basic salary of Mr. DeValois since 1937.

The mission suffered a great loss in the death of the first Mrs. DeValois in 1944. In 1946 Mr. DeValois married Miss Bernadine Siebers, M.D., a colleague of Dr. Ida Scudder at the Vellore Medical College. After three years of post-graduate study, Dr. DeValois was appointed in 1945 as professor in the department of ear, nose and throat at the Vellore Medical College. She has a dynamic Christian spirit, and the skill and efficiency needed to conduct her many-sided life as wife, professor, friend and advisor to the students at the Medical College and the Agricultural Institute, and to the poor and needy in the villages. The Bronxville Reformed Church Women's Society makes an annual contribution to Dr. (Mrs.) DeValois for her medical work.

In 1945 the Women's Society assumed responsibility

114

for the financial support of Miss Wilhelmina Jongewaard. Her home-making school for forty girls is at
Palmaner, South India, fifty-five miles from Vellore.
Besides conforming to the strict scholastic standards of
the Indian Government, Miss Jongewaard trains the
girls in home-making and practical farm work, co-
operating closely with Mr. DeValois' Agricultural
Institute. An Indian nurse, who is a trained midwife,
supported by the town of Palmaner, instructs the girls
in the care of the babies of mothers who must work in
the fields. Miss Jongewaard and her school girls are
famous for exquisite cross-stitched embroidery which
is in great demand all over India. When her graduates
return to their villages and marry, the sale of their
handiwork, through Miss Jongewaard's agency, en-
ables them to be free from coolie work in the fields, and
thus to improve the standard of living and child care
in their homes.

ARABIA

The Sheikdom of Kuwait is on the Persian Gulf,
one hundred miles south of Basrah. Having the only
good harbor on the eastern coast of Arabia, all the
world trade flowed through it to the interior of that
little-known peninsula. Some thirteen thousand boats,
built in Kuwait, went out each year to the pearl fish-
eries, where the divers lost their health, if not their
lives, and earned but the poorest wages.

Early in the century, Sheik Mubarrak of Kuwait was
influenced by an Arab friend to write to the Reformed

115

Church in America, requesting that they send a doctor and build a hospital, for which he gave a superb site.

In 1910 the first doctor and his wife, Dr. and Mrs. Stanley Mylrea, went there and took up residence in an Arab house. Gradually, during forty years of Christian patience, persistence and skill, living through tribal battles and world wars, the Mylreas and their colleagues won their way into the confidence of both the poorest and the richest of these unyielding Moslem people.

The Bronxville Reformed Church became interested in Kuwait fifty years ago, when in its Sunday School room there was placed a large drawing of a young man in Arab dress, to whom the children were sending their pennies. He was Ameen Effendi, a Syrian Christian, the first street preacher to go to Kuwait. He forfeited his life there, but he pointed the way to a door which was opening very slowly into Arabia.

The interest and support of the Bronxville Reformed Church have had a great part in this Christian enterprise from the beginning. Frank R. Chambers contributed the funds for the men's hospital which was built by Dr. Mylrea in 1913. This hospital, together with the women's hospital built in 1945, has ministered to many thousands of patients every year. For the past thirty years, the Bronxville Reformed Church Women's Society has annually provided the year's supply of surgical dressings, together with a considerable amount of bed linen and other hospital material for the Kuwait hospitals. Dr. and Mrs. Lewis R. Scudder and Dr. Mary B. Allison are looking forward to the building of a new hospital for men and the making of improvements in the hospital for women. These hospitals have never closed their books with a deficit. No matter how poor the Arabs are, they are asked to leave some token payment for the treatment received.

Confidence in the missionary doctors, such as Paul W. Harrison, Sharon J. Thoms, Wells Thoms and others, has grown through the years. Encouraged by the experience of the efficiency of western medicine and surgery, more and more people come to the mission hospital where they receive skillful treatment dispensed with Christian kindness. During World War II, thousands of American men in defense and government work, testified to the medical skill and Christian influence of these missionaries, throughout the Arab world.

IRAQ

The Tigris and Euphrates are rivers of Mesopotamia that flow through the background of history. They watered what was known as the Garden of Eden in the morning of time.

In 1902, a few years after the Arabian Mission was founded on the Persian Gulf, young John Van Ess came to Basrah at the crossroads of the world in the Tigris-Euphrates valley. He identified himself with the Arabs of town, country and river, and learned to speak fluently in the Arabic and Turkish languages. He studied deeply into the philosophy of the Moslem religion, and

117

the reasons for its grip on all phases of life and thought. Dr. Van Ess brought to rich and poor, official and laborer, a fresh, dynamic, practical interpretation of the new Gospel of Christ. Throughout his forty-seven years in the Near East, he was held in the highest esteem. He was a wise counselor, a fearless Christian, and an influential statesman throughout the Turkish regime, the first World War, the British Protectorate, the new Kingdom of Iraq and the second World War.

In 1911 Dr. Van Ess married Miss Dorothy Firman of Oak Park, Illinois. They were both personally identified for many years with the Bronxville Reformed Church through close ties of friendship.

In 1912 Dr. Van Ess started a school for boys at Basrah, called "High Hope." It now numbers 250 students and many of its graduates occupy high governmental, civil and commercial positions.

In the same year, Mrs. Van Ess founded the girls' school at Basrah, one of the first in that part of the Near East. The Women's Society of the Bronxville church has always shared in this work.

Farther up the Tigris River is the world renowned city of Bagdad, where the Reformed Church in America joined with other denominations in developing a united mission in Mesopotamia. A pressing need arose for the education of girls, and Mrs. Sharon J. Thoms, the widow of one of the early missionary doctors in Arabia, opened a school for them in 1925. Under difficult housing conditions and a shortage of teaching staff, Mrs. Thoms continued to maintain good educational

standards with real character training among Chris-
tion, Moslem and Jewish girls of many nationalities
until her retirement in 1945. The Bronxville Women's
Society was responsible for Mrs. Thoms' salary during
her active, valuable service in Iraq. It is gratifying that
the school, now numbering 225 pupils, is in an improved location and has more adequate housing.

The world wide interests of the Bronxville Reformed Church is a subject of great importance to all
its members, in the Church, Church School, Women's
Society and Men's Club.

"INTO ALL THE WORLD"

119

CHAPTER X

THE MEMORIALS

THE Reformed Church building is unusually rich in memorials. Dedicated to the Glory of God, and in memory of those who, by their lives of Christian service, have contributed to the quality of our civilization, these memorials add to the beauty of the church building, and aid in creating an atmosphere of spiritual contentment and quiet memory, essential to a place of worship.

THE MEMORIAL WINDOWS

The numbering of the windows, both aisle and clerestory, begins with those nearest the chancel on the south side of the church, and continues to the rear on that side; then crosses to the north side and continues towards the front, ending with clerestory window No. 10 nearest the chancel on the north side.

THE AISLE WINDOWS

The aisle windows develop the story of Christ's life, culminating in the large window in the chancel.

Designed in harmony with the Early English architecture of the church, the principal subjects are bordered by architectural canopies, while angelic figures kneel in attitudes of adoration in the base of each window panel; and angels with trumpets and censers, symbolizing Praise and Prayer, appear in the tracery which is enriched by decorative stars and clouds of heavenly glory.

FIRST WINDOW. The subjects of the two panels of the first aisle window are the Annunciation and the Nativity.

In the first, or right-hand panel, the angel of the Annunciation appears before the Blessed Virgin bearing the lily, symbol of purity, while brilliant rays of light emanate from the descending dove. The inscription reads, "Ave Maria, gratia plena."

In the field below is the symbol of the Expulsion from the Garden of Eden.

In the left panel, the Star of Bethlehem shines over the manger, with the ox and the ass and the Holy Family. Joseph bears his traditional flowering staff, and two musical angels kneel at the base.

121

This window was the gift of Mrs. Raymond S. Crawford in memory of her parents, and the inscription reads, "To the Glory of God and in Memory of William Bradford Homer and Louise Hart Homer."

SECOND WINDOW. The second window is devoted to the Adoration of the Magi, and the Presentation in the Temple.

In the right panel, the three kings kneel, with their gifts, around the Blessed Virgin and the Holy Child. A little symbol of Joseph with his staff is in the field nearby.

In the left panel, the ancient Simeon holds the Christ Child near the altar on which rests the seven-branched candlestick. Mary, with hands folded on her breast, and Joseph with the cage of doves, stand on either side of Simeon. There is a little figure of St. Paul, with his symbols, the book and the sword, suggesting his reference, "A Light to Lighten the Gentiles."

This window was the gift of Mr. and Mrs. Thomas B. Gilchrist in memory of their parents, and the memorial inscriptions read, "In memory of Frank Gilchrist and Minnie Whittemore Gilchrist," and "In memory of Samuel Boyd Goodman and Jennie Smith Goodman."

THIRD WINDOW. The third window represents Christ in the Temple and in the Carpenter Shop.

In the first panel, He is seated among the Doctors, while above, between the sanctuary lamps, is a little symbol of Joseph and Mary coming to find Him.

The left panel shows the Boy Christ working with His

father at the carpenter's bench. A symbol of Mary, His mother, spinning occurs in the field above. Below is a playful kitten, symbol of domestic felicity.

This window was the gift of Mr. James Roberton MacColl, Jr., in memory of his parents, and the inscription reads, "To the Glory of God and in Memory of James Roberton MacColl and Agnes Boyle MacColl."

FOURTH WINDOW. The subjects of the fourth window are the Baptism of Christ by Saint John, and the Temptation.

Above the Baptism is the descending Dove of the Holy Spirit, with issuing rays of Divine Strength.

Above the Temptation is the Hand of God from the clouds, and below the figure of the Tempter is the symbol of the Temple.

This window was the gift of Mr. Edgar S. Bowling, in memory of his father, and the inscription reads, "To the Glory of God and in Memory of Simeon Bowling."

FIFTH WINDOW. The right panel in the fifth window represents the Calling of the Disciples, Peter and Andrew, to be fishers of men. The little sailboat and the anchor, symbols of their occupation, embellish the field, while a white bird soars overhead.

The left panel represents the Sermon on the Mount. The eight saintly listeners, whose lives exemplify the qualities of the Beatitudes are, from the top down, Lazarus, the pure in spirit; Nicodemus, they that hunger and thirst after righteousness; Saint John the Evangelist, they that mourn; the Blessed Virgin, the meek; Saint Paul, the merciful; Saint John the Baptist, the persecuted; Saint Agnes, the clean of heart; and Saint Stephen, the peace makers. Above, appears the eight-pointed cross, symbol of the Beatitudes. The birds and lilies in the lower field symbolize tranquility.

This window was the gift of Mr. Arthur F. Corwin in memory of his wife, and the inscription reads, "To the Glory of God and in Memory of Claudia Thomas Corwin."

SIXTH WINDOW. The two panels of this window show Christ Blessing Little Children, and the Healing of the Sick.

In the first, the symbols of the birds and lamb with the children suggest Christ's love for small things.

In the second is the leper with his warning bell, and above is a suggestion of the multitude that came to hear and be healed by Christ.

This window was the gift of Mr. and Mrs. Ralph W. Gwinn, in memory of their daughter and the inscription reads, "To the Glory of God and in Memory of Margaret Harvey Gwinn."

SEVENTH WINDOW. The Triumphal Entry into Jerusalem and the Cleansing of the Temple are symbolized in the seventh window.

The small figures below Christ mounted on the colt are "They that went before, saying 'Hosannah! Blessed is He that cometh in the name of the Lord.'"

In the second panel, Christ is shown casting out the money-changers and the men who sold doves.

This window was the gift of Mrs. Ferris J. Meigs in memory of her husband, and the memorial inscription reads, "To the Glory of God and in Memory of Ferris J. Meigs."

EIGHTH WINDOW. The eighth and last aisle window is devoted to the Last Supper and the Trial Before Pilate.

In the right panel, Saint John, the Beloved Disciple, and Saint Peter are nearest the figure of Christ as He places the symbol of the wine before them.

In the left panel, the figure of Our Lord, clothed in the purple robe, wearing the crown of thorns, and bearing the palm in His bound hands, is surrounded by priests, mockers, soldiers and Pilate washing his hands.

This window was the gift of Mr. Jesse S. Phillips in memory of his wife, and the memorial inscription reads, "To the Glory of God and in Memory of Mary Cannon Phillips."

THE CHANCEL WINDOW

This window is designed to symbolize in the language of color and light, the Spirit of Christ triumphant throughout eternity, and His willing sacrifice for the redemption of mankind. "Greater love hath no man than this, that a man lay down his life for his friends." This final and supreme result of the life of Christ is the culmination of the series of significant incidents which are developed through the aisle windows.

The crucified Christ is represented in the lower central panel on a cross of ruby bordered with green, traditional color symbols of divine love and heavenly promise. In vertical arrangement beneath the arms of the cross are figures symbolical of all manner and races of mankind whom Christ came to redeem, indicating somewhat the chronological progress of Christianity throughout the world. Reading downward they represent — on the left side the Jew, first century; the Roman, second century; the Celt, third or fourth century; and the Chinese, nineteenth century: on the right side the Greek, first century; the Goth, medieval; the American Indian, primitive; and the African, nineteenth century.

At either side, above the arms, are the veiled sun and moon suggesting all Nature's acknowledgment of this world-stirring event.

The two mortals who were dearest to Him are in the panels at either side of the crucified Christ, His Blessed Mother and His Disciple Saint John. Above are their symbols, the vase of red roses of the Virgin and the eagle of the Evangelist.

In the center panel of the upper tier is the radiant figure of the enthroned Christ, always reigning in the hearts of men through His example and teaching. He is represented in a vesica of ruby and holds the symbol of His domination over the world, the globe surmounted by the cross.

In the side panels of the upper tier are adoring Cherubim and Seraphim, the choirs of angels nearest the throne of God. The ruby wings of the Seraphim symbolize divine love, and the blue wings of the Cherubim, heavenly contemplation. Flames of divine zeal enrich the blue fields, with emanating rays from the Divine Presence. Across the base of these panels is the text, "The kingdoms of this world are become the kingdoms of our Lord, and of Christ; and He shall reign for ever and ever."

Accented throughout the canopy are small figures related to the central themes. In the upper tier, musical angels, members of the angelic choir, join in the divine chorus of praise of the Creator. In the lower tier, reading downward in pairs, and beginning at the left side are Caiaphas, the High Priest; the Pharisee; Mary, mother of James; the Centurion, Joseph of Arimathea, Mary Magdalen, Nicodemus, the Penitent Thief, Saint Peter, Simon of Cyrene, Pilate, and Judas.

The uppermost tracery space bears the symbol of the Agnus Dei, the Lamb of God, with cruciform banner of triumph; while the smaller tracery spaces are enriched with stars and clouds of heavenly glory.

This chancel window was the gift of Mrs. A. J. Purdy, and the memorial inscription reads, "To the Glory of God and in Memory of Alexander Masterton, Jr., and Mary Hance Masterton. A tribute of their friend, Mary Legget Purdy."

THE CLERESTORY WINDOWS

The clerestory windows are each divided into three panels, their general design in harmony with the aisle windows below, and the subject matter taken from the stories of the Old Testament.

First Window. The three panels represent the Creation, the Fall and the Deluge.

In the right-hand panel, at either side of the symbol of the Creation, with the animals above and the fish below, are the blue-winged Cherubim and the red-winged Seraphim.

In the central panel, the Angel of Justice is the principal figure, above the traditional tree, serpent and Adam and Eve, with the figures of Eve spinning and Adam digging, at either side.

The left-hand panel shows the Ark with, at the sides, Noah building the Ark, and the return of the dove after the flood.

This window was the gift of Mr. and Mrs. Neal T. McKee, in memory of their son and of their nephew, and the memorial inscription reads, "In loving memory of Henry Clay McKee II and Ben Perry DeHaven."

Second Window. In the first panel of the second window, which is devoted to the great legendary figures of Abraham, Isaac and Jacob, Abraham is shown dividing the land with Lot. Represented at either side are the Departure of Lot, and the Sacrifice of Isaac.

The central panel is devoted to Isaac. In the center, the servant is bringing Rebekah to Isaac in the fields. At one side is shown Jacob with the kid, and at the other Jacob's deception of his father.

The left panel symbolizes Jacob with his twelve sons;

with his vision at Bethel on one side, and his wrestling with the angel at Peniel on the other.

This window was the gift of Mrs. A. J. Purdy, and the inscription reads, "To the Glory of God and in Memory of Jacob and Catharine Egbert."

THIRD WINDOW. The third window is devoted to the Egyptian Bondage; the right-hand panel showing Joseph in Egypt, ruler of the land under Pharaoh, building granaries in preparation for the famine. At the sides, Joseph is shown being sold into Egypt, and welcoming his family.

The central panel is dominated by Moses, with his rescue from the bulrushes symbolized below. The persecuted children of Israel working on the cities of Egypt, and the miracle of the burning bush are suggested on either side.

The left-hand panel shows the Deliverance under Moses, with the Crossing of the Red Sea and the destruction of the Egyptians indicated below the principal figure. On one side the Plagues are symbolized by ten arrows, and the Passover is symbolized on the other side.

This window was the gift of Mrs. F. Bradley Reynolds and her sons James Reynolds and Frederick Perry Reynolds in memory of her husband and their father. The inscription reads, "To the Glory of God and in Loving Memory of Francis Bradley Reynolds."

FOURTH WINDOW. This window is devoted to the Sojourn in the Wilderness, with Moses as the dominant figure.

In the first panel he is symbolized as the inspired deliverer and provider, through God, of sustenance and healing for his followers, with the miraculous gift of manna and quail shown below. On the right is shown the raising of the brazen serpent in the wilderness, and on the left the bringing forth of water from the rock of Horeb.

In the central panel Moses receives the tablets of the Law, and at the right is shown bearing them from Mount Sinai to his people below. At the left is the golden calf and its worshippers.

In the left-hand panel the High Priest Aaron and the worship of the Tabernacle is the dominant theme. On the right is shown the Israelites bringing gifts, and on the left Moses' vision of the promised land.

This window has not as yet been put in place.

FIFTH WINDOW. The Conquest of Canaan is the dominant theme of the fifth window.

The first panel is given over to Joshua, the warrior of God, and the fall of Jericho. Below is a symbol of the Ark of the Covenant being borne before the walls of the city. At the right Joshua crosses over the Jordan, and at the left he is confronted by the Captain of the Host of the Lord.

In the central panel, the figure of Samson stands above the symbol of his overthrow of the Temple of Dagon, and his own destruction with the host of the Philistines. At the right he bears the gates of Gaza, and at the left is Delilah with her shears.

PROPOSED NEW CHAPEL AND EDUCATION BUILDING

PROPOSED NEW CHAPEL AND EDUCATION BUILDING

The left-hand panel shows Samuel, priest and prophet, the last of the Judges, and the maker of Kings. Below he is symbolized seeking the chosen one among the sons of Jesse. At the right, the young Samuel serves Eli, and the anointing of Saul is shown at the left.

This window has not as yet been put in place.

SIXTH WINDOW. The sixth window symbolizes the United Kingdom.

In the first panel Saul is represented with shield and spear above the feast which Samuel prepared for him. To the right he is searching for his father's asses on the journey that led to his meeting with Samuel. At the left, he is symbolized battling with the Philistines.

The central panel shows David and his triumph over Goliath. At the right is the young shepherd, and at the left the sweet singer of Israel playing before Saul.

The left-hand panel commemorates Solomon. He holds a model of the Temple above a symbol of its building. His celebrated judgment between the two claimants of the child is at the right, and the Queen of Sheba at the left.

This window was the gift of Mrs. Margaret Ley Kent, Mrs. Roman G. Hubbell, and Mr. Harold Ley, Jr., the children of Mrs. Anne Kingsley Ley, in memory of their mother.

The memorial inscription reads, "To the Glory of God and in Loving Memory of Anne Kingsley Ley."

SEVENTH WINDOW. The seventh window symbolizes the division and decline of the Kingdom.

131

The first panel shows Rehoboam seated on his throne, and below are indicated the Twelve Tribes, divided ten against two, suggesting the Revolt and Division. At the right side Rehoboam refuses the counsel of the old men, and at the left Jeroboam is denounced by the Lord God of Israel.

The central panel celebrates the achievements of Elijah, with his triumph over the prophets of Baal as the dominant theme. He is shown being fed by ravens at the right, and dividing the waters with his mantle at the left.

The left-hand panel symbolizes the story of Amos, with the figure of the shepherd above the symbol of his prophecy of destruction in the center. His council of justice is suggested at the right, with the symbol of the scales above him. At the left is the symbol of his vision of the restoration of the Kingdom.

This window has not as yet been put in place.

EIGHTH WINDOW. The eighth window is devoted to three of the major prophets, the fourth, Daniel, being in the following or ninth window.

Isaiah dominates the right-hand panel, and below is shown the incident of the angel touching his lips with the fiery coal of divine purity and inspiration. At either side are symbols of his prophecy of the Suffering Servant, "wounded for our transgressions, bruised for our iniquities"; and the Coming of Christ's Kingdom.

Under the figure of Jeremiah in the central panel is a symbol of the breaking of his yoke by Hananiah as a sign of the release from bondage by Nebuchadnezzar. At the right is symbolized the call of Jeremiah when a child, with the vision of the almond tree, and at the left his imprisonment for prophecy.

The left-hand panel shows Ezekiel, and below his vision of the four-winged creatures with the faces of a man, a lion, an ox and an eagle, a suggestion of the traditional symbols of the four Evangelists, Matthew, Mark, Luke and John. Jonah is suggested at the right, sitting under his gourd outside the walls of Nineveh, and King Jehoiakim is suggested at the left.

This window has not as yet been put in place.

NINTH WINDOW. The ninth window is a symbol of the Babylonian captivity and the restoration under Persia.

In the right-hand panel Daniel is shown above a symbol of his experience in the lions' den. At the right is represented Daniel interpreting Nebuchadnezzar's dream, and at the left the decree of Darius.

The central panel shows Nehemiah with a symbol of the building of the Temple below. At the right he begs King Artaxerxes to send him into Judah, and at the left he looks upon the ruins of Jerusalem.

The left-hand panel is devoted to Esther. Below the figure of the Queen, is represented the banquet to which she invited the King and Haman. At the right are Mordecai and Haman at the King's gate and at the left Esther, accusing Haman.

The central and right-hand panels were the gift of Mrs. Chester M. Clark in memory of her father and mother, and the memorial inscriptions read, "In memory of Jessie Davis Fisher" and "In memory of Charles Everett Fisher."

The left-hand panel was the gift of Mr. Elmer C. Griffith in memory of his wife; and of his son Mr. Lewis Scott Griffith in memory of his mother. The memorial inscription reads, "In memory of Lucy Scott Griffith."

TENTH WINDOW. The tenth and last of the series of clerestory windows is given over to the Inter-Testament period.

In the first, or right-hand panel is shown the symbol of Alexander's conquest of the East, and the Ptolemies of Egypt. The small figure at the feet of Alexander is Antiochus Epiphanes, one of the Selucidae. Plato is shown on the right, and Aristotle on the left.

The central panel has Judas Maccabeus as the dominant figure, with Simon the High Priest of the later time shown below. On the right is Mattathias, and on the left Jonathan, the High Priest.

In the left-hand panel, Emperor Augustus is the principal figure, with King Herod represented below, thus leading up to the birth of Christ. On the right side is Pompey the Great, and on the left, Julius Caesar.

This window was the gift of a friend, and the memorial inscription reads, "To the Glory of God and in Loving Memory of Frank Dinsmore."

THE WAR MEMORIAL WINDOW

This window, in the church tower, was dedicated on Sunday, March 3, 1946. The service of dedication was conducted by the minister, Dr. John Henderson Powell, Jr., who spoke the following words:

"This morning we dedicate our War Memorial Window:

"To the glory of God, to the honor of all those from our parish who served in the armed forces of the United Nations, and in loving memory of those from our parish who gave their lives in this conflict with tyranny that we might live and enjoy the blessings of freedom.

"This window is therefore dedicated as an enduring tribute to the devotion and valor of all those whose names appear upon our Honor Roll, and especially to these eighteen who lost their lives in the service of our country:

"Roger G. B. Broome, III
Helene Wack Burnett
Richard Hunter Field
Karl D. Gardner
Robert A. Johnson
Richard Robinson Major
Clifford M. Markle
Robert R. O'Loughlin, Jr.
Edward E. Quimby

Carl W. Sautter
Howard Cotterill Sheperd, Jr.
Bruce Kingsley Stowell
Loring Thompson
Charles A. Tier
J. Carter Treadwell
Douglas Byrd Van Buskirk
A. Mangum Webb
Robert P. Wilson"

The window was designed to symbolize in color and light, the Christian virtues, and especially the qualities of Courage, Heroism and Sacrifice in the cause of Liberty and Freedom.

The theme, from the 16th verse of the 118th Psalm, is in the text running across the lancets, "The right hand of the Lord is exalted; the right hand of the Lord doeth valiantly."

This thought is personified in the principal figures representing the Old Testament warriors of Jehovah — Joshua, with his spear and shield, and David with sling and frail staff, in the central panels.

In the outer panels are the Archangels, Saint Michael with his flaming sword and shield, Captain of the Hosts of Heaven; and Saint Gabriel with his trumpet, Messenger of Peace and Glad Tidings.

The predellas are related to the figures above. Below Saint Michael is a symbol of his triumph over the dragon. Joshua commands the seven priests with their seven trumpets, and protects the Ark of the Covenant, the shattered walls of Jericho being in the background. The inspired David defies the giant Goliath; and the Angel Gabriel brings his glad tidings to the Shepherds of Bethlehem.

The tracery spaces are devoted to the Nine Choirs of Angels, "The Company of Heaven and all the Powers therein." These are in turn subdivided into three groups of Choirs — the Councillors, the Governors and the Messengers.

The Councillors are in the position of first importance being ranged at either side of the central symbol of the Cross, in pairs. The Governors are below and the Messengers at right and left.

Of the Choir of Councillors, the ruby-winged Seraphim, nearest the Cross, bear hearts symbolical of Divine Love. The blue-winged Cherubim have open books signifying Divine Wisdom, and the Thrones hold symbols of the Seat of Heavenly Grace.

Of the Choir of Governors, Dominations are represented in the two central panels below, with their symbols, the swords. Virtues, at the left (one panel) bear
the spear, and Powers at the right (one panel) hold the
dragon in chains. The Choir of Messengers are symbolized in the four outer panels of this tier.

The Principalities, with their lily symbol, are in two
panels, with archangels at extreme left bearing the
scales, and angels at the extreme right with the censer.

The smaller tracery spaces above the lancets are enriched with six-pointed stars of the Old Testament, and
five-pointed stars of the New Testament, the symbolism
being completed in the smaller spaces with flames and
stars of inspired zeal and heavenly glory.

This window was the joint gift of approximately
nine hundred members and friends of the church, who
contributed to the fund for its installation. The names
of the contributors are recorded in the Book of Remembrance and may be found in the Appendix, Part 17, of
this volume.

The general scheme of the entire series of the memorial windows was devised and developed by the minister, Dr. John Henderson Powell, Jr., who also worked
out the iconography of the individual windows as well
as that of the entire group.

The windows were designed and fabricated by
Charles J. Connick Associates of Boston, Massachusetts,
under the immediate direction of Harry Leslie Walker,
the architect of the building.

THE BELLS

The bells in the Tower are in memory of the Rev. Otis Tiffany Barnes, and were the gift of Ralph W. Gwinn. They were cast in Loughborough, England by John Taylor and Son, one of the oldest and most noted bell founders in the world. A memorial plate set in the wall of the narthex bears the following inscription, "The bells in the Tower above, were given in memory of Otis Tiffany Barnes, Minister of this church from April 1, 1916 to February 20, 1919."

The late Rev. Dr. James Coffin Stout made and played arrangements of some two hundred hymn tunes on the eight bells, which range in size from a diameter of eighteen inches to that of five feet. Many of Dr. Stout's arrangements are still being used, and they are, in a sense, themselves a memorial to him.

THE ORGAN

The organ, in memory of Mrs. James Lovejoy Robertson, was given by members of her family and her friends. The inscription on the memorial plate placed on the organ console reads, "This organ is in loving memory of Margaret Elizabeth Robertson, wife of the Rev. James Lovejoy Robertson, D.D., Minister of this Church, 1903-1915."

THE ORGAN SCREEN

The organ screen was the gift of Mary Legget Young, (the present Mrs. A. J. Purdy) and the inscription on

138

the memorial plate reads, "This organ screen is in loving memory of Alexander Masterton, Jr., Elder from 1850 until his death, May 3, 1899."

THE PULPIT, LECTERN AND CHANCEL RAIL

The pulpit, lectern and chancel rail were the gift of Mary and Hugh Robertson in memory of their father. The inscription on the pulpit reads, "In memory of Rev. James Lovejoy Robertson, D.D., beloved pastor of this Church 1903-1915."

THE ELDERS' SEATS AND PANELLING

The elders' seats and adjoining panelling at the rear of the Chancel were the gift of Miss Amie S. Dusenberry. The inscription on the memorial plate reads, "These Elders' seats are in memory of Alexander and Euphenus Masterton and their children: — Robert M. Masterton, Alexander Masterton, Jr., Mary M. Dusenberry, John M. Masterton."

THE COMMUNION TABLE

The communion table in the old church had been given by Mrs. Francis Bacon, in memory of her husband, Francis Bacon. When the present church was built, the new communion table was given by Mr. Bacon's family, and in its top was set the memorial plate removed from the former table. The inscription on the plate reads, "To the Glory of God and in Memory of Francis Bacon, member of the Consistory of this church from October 9, 1873 until his death December 20, 1905. 'Thou wilt keep him in perfect peace.'"

THE COMMUNION TABLE LINEN

The monogrammed linen table cloths used at communion services have long been provided by the family of Robert Alexander Hamilton. Mr. Hamilton himself supplied the cloths during his lifetime, and after his death Mrs. Hamilton gave a new one in his memory. Later a new monogrammed linen table cloth was given in memory of their parents, Mr. and Mrs. Robert Alexander Hamilton by their children, Dr. and Mrs. Arthur C. Allison and Mr. and Mrs. Herbert D. Hamilton.

THE CROSS

The Cross on the Communion Table, designed and fabricated by Lamont A. Warner, made of silver and set with semi-precious stones, and given by him in memory of his wife who died in 1923, is inscribed on one side "Holy, Holy, Holy, Lord God of Hosts," and on the reverse, "To the Glory of God and in Loving Memory of Emma Victorine Warner. 1876-1923. 1927."

THE FLOWER VASES

The brass flower vases used on the communion table were the gift of Mrs. A. L. Warnshuis, and the inscription reads, "In happy memory of Elias Warner Dusenberry and his beautiful arrangements of flowers for many years. Given by Margaret Chambers Warnshuis, October 28, 1947."

THE FONT AND FONT COVER

The baptismal font which was brought from the old church had been given by a former minister, the Rev. Edward J. Runk in memory of his wife, and it is marked "In memoriam, Idae Augustae Runk, 1883." The new marble base beneath the font, and the carved wood font cover above were the gift of Frank Dinsmore in memory of his nephew. The memorial brass plate reads, "This font cover is in loving memory of Alfred Dinsmore Bunz."

THE FOUNDERS' TABLET

On the wall of the narthex is the white marble Founders' Tablet, placed there when the present church building was erected, the gift of Miss Amie S. Dusenberry. The inscription reads, "1850-1926. In Pious Memory of Edward R. Hunt, James M. Prescott, Ann R. Prescott, Ellen M. Prescott, Euphenus Masterton, Alexander Masterton, Jr., Catharine Welbasky, James P. Swain, Catharine E. Swain, Margaret Harper, Mary Morison, Jean Morison, who founded this church on November 5, 1850."

THE MASTERTON TABLET

Colored glass windows which were removed when the old church building was taken down had been placed there in memory of Alexander Masterton, Jr. To take their place, a bronze portrait tablet was placed on the south wall of the new building, the inscription reading, "1850-1899. In loving memory of Alexander Masterton, who served this church as Deacon and as Elder from its organization until his death."

THE PRESCOTT TABLET

In the south aisle is a marble tablet placed there in memory of James M. Prescott, one of the founders of this church, and an officer of many years' service. This tablet is the gift of his relatives, Col. and Mrs. Lewis S. Latimer, and the inscription reads, "In memory of James Minot Prescott, 1797-1874. An Elder in this church 1850-1860. Superintendent of Sunday School 1850-1874."

THE MARBLE SLAB OVER THE CRYPT

When the present church building was erected, the interments in the burying ground adjoining the old church were removed, and placed in a sealed crypt under the nave of the new church. In the floor above the crypt was placed a marble slab recording this action. The inscription on the slab reads as follows: — " 'That He might be Lord of both the dead and the living.' In the vault beneath this stone, lie the earthly remains of those who were buried in the churchyard, 1850-1900." The names recorded on the stone may be found in the Appendix, Part 14.

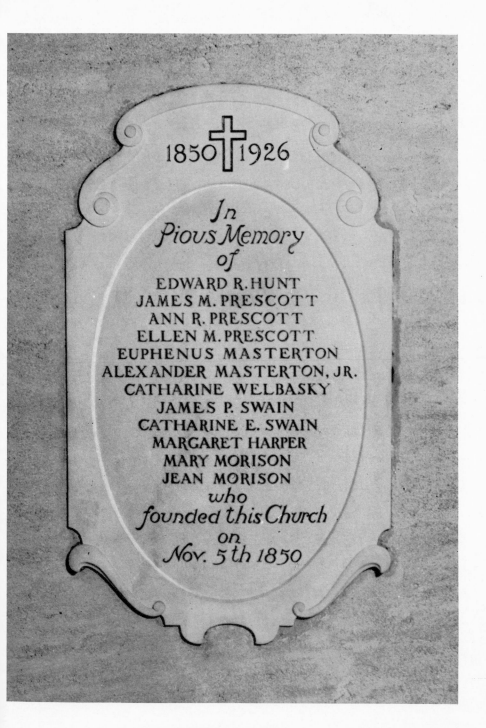

FOUNDERS TABLET

BAPTISMAL FONT

THE CHAMBERS TABLET

In the north aisle is a marble tablet in honor of Frank R. Chambers, the gift of his daughters, Mrs. William Clark Hawkins and Mrs. A. Livingston Warnshuis. The inscription reads, "In memory of Frank Ross Chambers, 1850-1940. Leader of Men, Beloved of Children, Faithful Servant of the Church."

THE ROBERTSON TABLET

When the portrait tablet in memory of Mr. Masterton was placed on the south wall, a similar one in memory of Dr. Robertson was placed on the north wall, the inscription reading, "In memory of Rev. James Lovejoy Robertson, D.D. Beloved pastor of this church for 12 years. 1903-1915."

THE BARNES TABLET

On the wall of the north aisle, is a bronze tablet in memory of the Rev. Mr. Barnes, a former minister of this church, who died from an illness contracted while doing war work during the first World War. The inscription reads, "In loving memory of Otis Tiffany Barnes, pastor of this church from April 1, 1916 until his death, February 20, 1919."

THE MEMORIAL PEWS

At the time of the erection of the present church building, many of the pews were given as memorials for friends or relatives of the donors. In a majority of cases small brass plates, recording these gifts, were placed on the pews.

A list of the memorial pews follows:

Francis Bacon, Esq.
 The gift of Mrs. Francis Bacon and family

Robert Louis Calkins, 1856-1926
 The gift of Mrs. Robert Louis Calkins

Almira LaDue Comfort, 1868-1913
 The gift of Mrs. Robcliff V. Jones
 in memory of her mother

Mrs. Samuel Hanson Cox (Anna Bacon)
 The gift of Mrs. Francis Bacon and family

Isadore Douglas Coyle, 1888-1927
 The gift of the Women's Society of the
 Reformed Church of Bronxville

Mary M. Dusenberry, 1829-1911
 The gift of Miss Amie S. Dusenberry
 in memory of her mother

William Henry Dusenberry, 1823-1866
Mary Anne Dusenberry, 1823-1902
 The gift of Mr. and Mrs. Walter E. Hallett
 in memory of Mrs. Hallett's parents

Jacob Egbert, 1861-1924

Kate Uglow Elliott, 1858-1925
Arthur Henry Elliott, 1851-1918
 The gift of Mrs. W. Armstrong Smith
 in memory of her parents

Bethia Wells Entwisle, 1838-1889
 The gift of E. B. Entwisle
 in memory of his mother

Anna Marshall Evans, 1842-1894
The gift of Harry M. Evans
in memory of his mother

William and Imogen Granberry

Alese Jeffress Harris
The gift of Mrs. Hugh S. Robertson
in memory of her sister

Heimerle
The gift of Mr. and Mrs. George Heimerle
in memory of their parents

Imrie
Malcolm Imrie, 1833-1897 (father)
Margaret B. Smyth Imrie, 1845-1918 (mother)
Lillie Catharine Imrie, 1873-1919 (sister)
Ebenezer Robert Imrie, 1880-1893 (brother)
Malcolm George Imrie, 1886-1918 (brother)
The gift of Isabelle Imrie, Margaret B. Imrie,
and their cousin, Madeline Smyth, in memory

James Ira Jones, 1842-1922
The gift of Robcliff V. Jones
in memory of his father

Alexander Masterton 2nd, 1825-1899
Mary Augusta Hance Masterton, 1823-1907
The gift of Mrs. William Nelson Ferris
in memory of her parents

Alexander Masterton 3rd, 1857-1858
Joseph Earle Masterton, 1860-1867
The gift of Mrs. William Nelson Ferris
in memory of her brothers

Alexander Milne, 1832-1915
The gift of Mrs. Alexander Milne

Charlotte Elizabeth Ogilvie, 1848-1924
The gift of John S. Ogilvie
in memory of his mother

James M. Prescott, 1797-1874
The gift of Mrs. Mary E. Latimer and family
in memory of her great-uncle

William Phillips Rae, Jr., 1900-1920
The gift of Mrs. William P. Rae

Stephen Roeser, 1826-1912
Wilhelmina Roeser, 1836-1923
The gift of John E. Roeser
in memory of his parents

Frederick Edmund Signer, 1869-1923
The gift of Dorothy Signer and Marjorie Signer
in memory of their father

Gertrude Canfield Smith, 1850-1916
The gift of Howard V. Smith
in memory of his mother

Albanus Hallowell Snyder, 1841-1893
Clara Manderson Snyder, 1844-1890
The gift of Mrs. John E. Roeser
in memory of her parents

William Shaw Stewart, M.D., 1838-1903
The gift of Mrs. George W. Barr
in memory of her father

Margaret Augusta Taylor, 1846-1914
The gift of Mrs. Charles D. Ryan
in memory of her mother

John Alfred Van Steenbergh
Mary Ann Van Steenbergh
The gift of Ella Van Steenbergh
in memory of her parents

THE AMERICAN FLAGS

The American Flag which hangs in the nave of the church and the American Flag in the assembly hall of the Bible School, were given by Frank Dinsmore, in memory of his sister, Sarah Kraft.

THE UNITED NATIONS FLAG

The Flag of the United Nations is in memory of William Leonard Colt, member of the Consistory of this church, the gift of Mrs. William Leonard Colt.

Two other flags hanging in the nave, while not memorials in the sense of being in honor of a certain individual or group of individuals, would seem to be appropriately mentioned in this chapter:

THE CHURCH FLAG

The church flag was a gift, in gratitude to the church, from Luther McConnell, a former member of the Consistory, when he moved with his family from Bronxville.

THE REFORMED PROTESTANT DUTCH CHURCH FLAG

The flag of the Reformed Protestant Dutch Church, with its beautiful and interesting coat of arms upon a white ground, signifies the honored parentage of our local church. It was the gift of Frank Dinsmore.

147

THE SERVICE FLAGS

Hanging in the nave of the church are two service flags, the one for World War I having twenty blue stars on a white field; and the one for World War II having the figure 18 beneath the gold star, and the figure 352 beneath the blue star.

ROLL OF HONOR, WORLD WAR I

Originally hung on the wall of the old church building, and now in the narthex of the present church, is the bronze tablet commemorating those members of the Reformed Church parish who were in active service during World War I. The wording of the tablet is as follows: — "In honor of the members of the Parish of the Reformed Church of Bronxville who served their country in its military and naval forces during the World War 1914-1918. 'Thanks be to God who giveth us the Victory.'" There follows a list of the names of the individuals so honored, which may be found in the Appendix, Part 15.

ROLL OF HONOR, WORLD WAR II

Also in the narthex of the church is the Roll of Honor of those who were in active service during World War II. The inscription reads, "Roll of Honor. The Reformed Church, Bronxville, N. Y. Members of the Parish who are serving in the Armed Forces of the United Nations. 1941-1945." The list of names on the World War II Roll of Honor may be found in the Appendix, Part 16.

148

PEW FROM OLD MIDDLE DUTCH CHURCH, NEW YORK

There is now preserved in the church, one of the original pews of the old church, first used in the Middle Dutch Church in New York. The inscription on the memorial plate reads, "This pew, first used during pre-Revolutionary days in the old Middle Dutch Church Nassau Street, New York City, was among those brought to Bronxville in 1850 when that church was demolished, to furnish the first building of the Protestant Reformed Dutch Church then being erected on this site."

BIBLE SCHOOL LECTERN

The lectern in the assembly room of the Bible School bears a plate inscribed, "In loving memory of Edward A. Yungel, who served in this Church School for seven years."

BIBLE SCHOOL ALTAR CLOTH

The altar cloth on the table of the worship center in the assembly room of the Bible School was given in memory of Mrs. H. Lewis Dudley, Jr., by Mr. Dudley and their daughters, Anne Gilbert Dudley and Dorothy Brown Dudley.

WORSHIP CENTER IN KINDERGARTEN

Above the worship center in the kindergarten room is a picture, "Jesus with the Children," and on the table

149

are two brass vases and an offering plate, all given in memory of Pearle Boyd Bascom.

PRIMARY CLASS ROOMS FURNISHINGS

The furnishings of one of the primary department class rooms were given by Margaret Chambers Halsey (the present Mrs. A. L. Warnshuis) in memory of her brother William Waller Chambers, 1885-1897. After his death, his parents, Mr. and Mrs. Frank R. Chambers had built in 1898 as a memorial to him the primary department class room addition to the original building on the site of the present church.

The furnishings of another of the primary department class rooms were given by Mr. A. H. White in memory of his grandson, Alvord White Clements.

SUNDAY SCHOOL ROOM OF OLD CHURCH

It should be noted that in the year 1873, Alexander Masterton, Jr., had built and furnished a Sunday School room as an addition to the old church building, in memory of his two sons, Alex and Joseph E., who had recently died.

COLLECTION PLATES AND COMMUNION SERVICE

A local newspaper, dated December 11, 1920, gives some interesting data as follows. The collection plates in use at that time and bearing the date 1907, had been given by Mrs. William Nelson Ferris in memory of her deceased parents, Mr. and Mrs. Alexander Masterton,

Jr. A further item states that on June 21, 1851, Mr. Masterton gave a silver communion service to the church, each member of his family having given one piece of the set. On February 9, 1879, when the residence of Mr. Masterton was destroyed by fire, this communion service was lost. Mr. Masterton then provided another one which was used until January, 1903, when the individual communion cups now in use in the church began to be used. The tankard and four goblets have been carefully preserved, and one of the goblets is now used, symbolically, upon the communion table, whenever the Lord's Supper is celebrated.

THE CLOISTER AND THE CLOISTER GARDEN

The Cloister and the planting of the Cloister garden were given by Margaret Chambers Halsey in memory of her husband, Charles Woodruff Halsey. Incised in a marble tablet, set in one of the Cloister piers is the inscription, "This cloistered walk and the garden within are a memorial to the life of Charles Woodruff Halsey. 1877-1925."

THE DOGWOOD TREE

The dogwood tree on the lawn south of the church tower was given in memory of Elias W. Dusenberry by the working gardeners of Bronxville.

THE APPENDIX

———◆———

THE APPENDIX

1

THE NAME OF THE CHURCH

AT the first meeting of the Consistory of the Bronxville Church, held December 14, 1850, a resolution was adopted "That the name or title by which we and our successors forever hereafter shall be known and distinguished as a body corporate is 'The Reformed Protestant Dutch Church of Bronxville.'" At the same meeting a resolution was passed "That the seal here presented with the impression of a Bible enclosed by a circle and around this enclosed in another circle the letters 'R D Church Bronxville' be the corporate seal of the Church." When the actual design for the seal was made, the name was spelled out in full, — "Reformed Protestant Dutch Church, Bronxville, N. Y." Since that time the name of the Bronxville Church has remained unchanged, notwithstanding the change which later took place in the name of the church denomination in America.

Previous to 1867, the denomination in America was known as "Reformed Dutch Church" or "The Reformed Protestant Dutch Church." The denomination had been incorporated in 1819 under the latter name. In 1867, after a somewhat heated discussion, the name of the denomination was changed by General Synod to "The Reformed Church in America." This action was approved by Act of the Legislature of the State of New York in 1869. It was, nevertheless, provided by the General Synod at the time the name of the denomination was thus changed, that the name of a local church, whatever it was before 1867, should remain unimpaired by the change of the name of the church denomination.

Therefore, while the official name of the Bronxville church continues to be that of the extended form, it is now customary to use the shorter form, "The Reformed Church of Bronxville."

2

THE ORGANIZATION OF THE REFORMED
CHURCH IN AMERICA

THIS is the form of the organization of the Reformed Protestant Dutch Church — now known as the Reformed Church in America

155

— as planned by Dr. John Henry Livingston of Rutgers College, and as adopted by the church in 1791. The organization exists in this form today.

The local congregation is governed by a Consistory composed of elders and deacons chosen from the male adult members of the church, and elected for a period of two years each, the terms of office of only one half of them expiring in any one year. They, with the minister, who is by virtue of his office, president of the Consistory, have full charge of the affairs and interests of the congregation. The minister (who is a *preaching elder*, in contradistinction to the others, who are *ruling elders*) and the elders have charge of the definitely spiritual interests of the congregation. They receive, dismiss, rebuke and excommunicate members, and represent the congregation in the higher judicatories. The deacons have charge of the temporalities of the church, and especially the care of the poor. Church properties are acquired, held or disposed of, by and in the name of the Consistory.

The next higher governing body is the Classis, composed of a minister and one elder from each church within a certain area. The Classis meets twice each year and may meet oftener if necessary. It has general supervision of the group of churches, advises upon the choice of ministers for vacant churches, approves calls, ordains candidates and installs pastors. It is also a court of appeal from decisions of a Consistory. The Reformed Church of Bronxville is in the Classis of Westchester.

Above the Classis is the Particular Synod, which is composed of a number of Classes within a designated area. Two ministers and two elders from each Classis in this area are named each year to be delegates to this Synod. They review the acts of the Classes and elect delegates to the General Synod.

It is also a court of appeal from the decisions of a Classis.

The supreme judicatory of the Reformed Church is the General Synod which meets annually. It is composed of ministers and elders from the various Classes, varying according to the number of church members in the Classis. These delegates are nominated by the Classes and are elected by the Particular Synod. The General Synod reviews the work of the whole church, of its benevolent Boards (Education, Missionary and Relief), initiates policies and authorizes activities, interprets the Constitution, legislates for the denomination and is the final court of appeal.

The work of the church is administered through the following boards:

1. The Board of Direction is the custodian of the funds of General Synod including the endowments of its seminaries.

2. The Board of Education labors in the area of student aid, recruiting for the ministry, Christian education and work with the institutions of the church.

3. The Board of Domestic Missions aids small or weak churches, seeks to establish others where needed, labors among the Negroes of the South, the Italians and Hungarians of large cities, and joins with the Women's Board of Domestic Missions in work among the Indians and the Mountaineers.

4. The Board of Foreign Missions maintains missions in China, India, Japan, Arabia and Mesopotamia.

5. The Church Building Fund aids in erecting buildings for new churches.

6. The Board of Publication and Bible School Work issues denominational literature, takes leadership in religious education and evangelism, and maintains a book depository.

7. The Disabled Minister's Fund provides relief for ministers who are in need.

8. The Widow's Fund provides for the care of widows and children of ministers.

9. The Women's Board of Foreign Missions cooperates with the Board of Foreign Missions in work among women and children.

10. The Women's Board of Domestic Missions assists in building and equipping parsonages and churches and maintains missions among immigrants, Indians, Negroes, and Kentucky Mountaineers.

11. The Minister's Fund consists of an endowment of a million dollars which is used for ministerial pensions.

In addition to these, the Reformed Church in America aids the American Bible Society and other worthy agencies. The offices of the Boards of the Reformed Church in America are at 156 Fifth Avenue, New York.

The spirit of the church is exemplified in its conviction of the universality of the gospel and its desire and efforts to share the work of the world in cultivating the spiritual life, thereby bringing about the Kingdom of God.

3

THE NAME BRONXVILLE

As THE Reformed Dutch Church came to us from the Netherlands, so the name Bronxville came to us indirectly from the same source.

On a day in July, 1639 a holiday was proclaimed in New Amsterdam by William Kieft, the governor, to welcome the arrival of the ship "De Brantvan Trogen" out of Amsterdam, Holland.

Jonas Bronck, owner of the vessel, was a native of Denmark, well educated, and a man of culture. In his young manhood he journeyed to Holland in search of greater freedom of thought and religion. There he married Antonia Slagboome, daughter of a wealthy merchant. The newly married couple lived in Hoorn for a time, and it was there that the idea of voyaging to the new world was developed.

With the help of Bronck's father-in-law a ship was purchased, provisioned, loaded with farm implements, cattle, seed, household goods and other articles necessary to establish a homestead in a new land. The ship also carried a number of servants, and men skilled in agriculture and the care of livestock.

Bronck must have been pleased with the warm welcome he received from the people in New Amsterdam. He began immediate negotiations for the purchase from the Indians of a five hundred-acre tract in the southern part of Westchester. It was located between the Harlem and Aliquaburg (Bronck's) rivers, in the neighborhood of Lincoln Avenue and East 132nd Street, later called Morrisania.

It was not long before Bronck acquired title to the land by deed signed by the Indian Sachems Ramaque and Tackamuck. He erected a dwelling house of stone, barns, barracks and a tobacco house. The completed farm was named Aninomus. From time to time Bronck acquired more land. He established a grist mill on the Aliquaburg River flowing through his property, three miles from its mouth.

Jonas Bronck was destined to enjoy his new home for only four short years. He died in 1643, the first recorded white settler in the area. He left a well-developed plantation, a grist mill, a library of twenty printed volumes, eighteen pamphlets and sixteen books in manuscript. Among his other assets were table silver, napkins, tablecloths and six linen shirts.

In the course of time the Aliquaburg River became known as Bronck's River from its headwaters north of Kensico to its confluence with the Harlem River. The accepted spelling became Bronx.

As the Bronx River flowed through the property of James P. Swain, he is credited with suggesting the name "Bronxville" for the little settlement then called Underhill's Crossing.

Later, this name was officially sanctioned by the United States Government when a post office was established on July 20, 1852, with Lancaster O. Underhill, a faithful member of the Reformed Church, as postmaster.

4

MINISTERS

ACKERLY, GEORGE ASA

b. Brooklyn, N. Y., October 13, 1897
Wesleyan Univ., A.B., 1920; Union Theological Seminary, 1921
Yale Divinity School, B.D., 1924
Director Religious Education, Second Presbyterian Church, Amsterdam, N. Y., 1925-26
Principal Boys' Community School, Arrah, Bihar, India, 1926-31
Ordained, Lucknow, India, 1928
Minister, Congregational Church, Mansfield Center, Conn., 1931-37
Associate Minister, Mt. Pleasant Congregational Church, Washington, D. C., 1937-40
Minister, First Federated Church, Templeton, Mass., 1940-45
Associate Minister, Reformed Church, Bronxville, 1945-50
Associate Minister, Church of the Covenant, Cleveland, Ohio, 1950-

BARNES, OTIS TIFFANY

b. Philadelphia, Pa., September 18, 1885
Lafayette College, 1909; Union Theological Seminary, 1912
Minister, Congregational Church, Chappaqua, N. Y., 1912-16
Minister, Reformed Church, Bronxville, 1916-19
Publications: *Children's Object Story Sermons*
d. Bronxville, February 20, 1919

BRYAN, ROBERT R.

b. Pennsylvania, 1889
Princeton University, A.B., 1910
Princeton Seminary, A.M., 1915
Graduate study, University of Nebraska, Union Theological
Seminary, Oxford University
Sterling College, Sterling, Kan., D.D., 1923
Minister, Central United Presbyterian Church, Omaha, Neb.,
1923-30
Minister, Church of the Messiah, Paterson, N. J., 1930-45
Interim Minister, Presbyterian Church, Rye, N. Y., 1947
Interim Minister, Reformed Church, Bronxville, February-
June, 1950

COLLIER, JOSEPH A.

b. Plymouth, Mass., October 26, 1828
Rutgers College, 1849
New Brunswick Seminary, 1852
Minister, Greenville Reformed Church and Bronxville, 1852-55
Minister, Reformed Church, Geneva, N. Y., 1855-59
Minister, Second Reformed Church, Kingston, N. Y., 1859-64
Publications: *The Young Men of the Bible, The Dawn of
Heaven* and a prize essay on peace, *The Right Way*
d. August, 1864

DeVRIES, J. HENDRICK

b.Amsterdam, Netherlands, May 8, 1859
Rutgers College, 1881
New Brunswick Seminary, 1888
Licensed by Classis of Westchester; ordained by Presbytery of
Westchester, 1888
Missionary pastor Immanuel Chapel, Yonkers, N. Y., 1888-93
Minister, Reformed Church, Bronxville, 1893-97
Minister, Second Presbyterian Church, Princeton, N. J., 1897-
1905
Rutgers College, D.D., 1903
Publications: Translation from Dutch, one vol. Dr. Kuyper's
Encyclopedia of Sacred Theology, 1898; Articles for Religious
Press

DITZEN, LOWELL RUSSELL

b. Kansas City, Kan., 1913
Park College, Parkville, Mo.
William Jewell College, Liberty, Mo., 1933
McCormick Theological Seminary, Chicago, Ill., B.D., 1936
Graduate study at Divinity School of University of Chicago
    and at Union Theological Seminary in New York
Park College, D.D., 1943
Minister, Pullman Presbyterian Church, Chicago, 1934-38
Minister, South Shore Presbyterian Church, Chicago, 1938-42
Assistant Minister, Brick Presbyterian Church, New York,
    1942-43
Minister, First Presbyterian Church, Utica, N. Y., 1943-50
Exchange Preacher, Federated Council of Churches in Eng-
    land, Scotland and France, 1948; German Refugee Camps,
    Germany, 1949
Minister, Reformed Church, Bronxville, 1950-

EDWARDS, DEANE

b. St. Paul, Minn., March 31, 1885
Princeton University, A.B., 1906
Auburn Theological Seminary graduate, 1912
Auburn Fellowship English Universities, 1912-13
Ordained Presbyterian Church, 1913
Minister, Seneca Falls, N. Y., 1913-18
Chaplain, U. S. Army, 1918-19
Minister, Reformed Church, Bronxville, 1919-29
Minister, The Church in Radburn, Fairlawn, N. J., 1929-35
Associate Director, National Preaching Mission, 1936-37
Federal Council of Churches, 1937-50
Member World Conference on Church, Community and State,
    Oxford, England, 1937
Member World Conference on Faith and Order, Edinburgh,
    Scotland, 1937
President, Hymn Society of America, 1948-
Author and Editor various pamphlets on Worship
National Council of Churches of Christ in U. S. A., 1950-

HEATH, WILLIAM THOMAS

b. Chicago, Ill., January 17, 1898
Princeton University, A.B., 1920
Auburn Theological Seminary graduate, 1925
Auburn Fellowship to Oxford University, England, 1926
Ordained Buffalo Presbytery, 1925
Assistant Minister, Reformed Church, Bronxville, 1926-27
Minister, West Center Congregational Church, Bronxville, 1927-33
Ordained Deacon, 1933; Priest, 1934 (Episcopal)
Assistant Rector, Trinity Episcopal Church, Buffalo, N. Y., 1933-36
Rector, Trinity Church, Buffalo, 1936-
Union Theological Seminary, S.T.M., 1949

HUTCHINS, JOHN

b. Portsmouth, England, June 29, 1848
Wisconsin University, 1873
Western Theological Seminary, Allegheny, Pa., 1873-75
Union Theological Seminary, 1875-76
Ordained by Classis of Westchester, November 28, 1876
Minister, Reformed Church, Bronxville, 1876-82
Minister, Ellenville, N. Y., 1882-87; Brighton Heights, 1887-92
Minister, Middle Collegiate Church, New York, 1892-95
Minister, Congregational Church, Litchfield, Conn., 1895-1915
d. February 20, 1915

MacLEAN, HUGH BAILLIE

b. Shetland Islands
St. Andrew's University, Scotland
St. Andrew's Theological Seminary, Scotland
Union Theological Seminary, New York, Th.D.
Chaplain Royal Air Force, six years
Professor Old Testament, New Brunswick Theological Seminary
Interim Minister, Reformed Church, Bronxville, July and August, 1950

MacQUEEN, PETER

b. Wigtonshire, Scotland, January 11, 1863
College of New Jersey, 1887
Union Theological Seminary, New York, 1890
Ordained by Classis of Westchester, May 14, 1891
Minister, Reformed Church, Bronxville, 1891-93
Minister, Congregational Church, Somerville, Mass., 1893
d. Boothbay Harbor, Me., January 10, 1924

McCANCE, WILLIAM H.

b. Edgewood, Pa.
Yale University, A.B., 1918
Yale Divinity School, B.D., 1921
Congregational missionary in Bombay, India, 1921-29
Associate Secretary, Foreign Missions Conference
Associate Minister, First Congregational Church, Stamford, Conn.
Assistant Minister, Reformed Church, Bronxville, 1933-38
Minister, Congregational Church, Middlebury, Conn., 1938-43 and 1945-48
Chaplain, U. S. Army, 1943-45
Minister, First Congregational Church, Long Beach, Calif., 1948-

McNEUR, RONALD WILLIAM

b. Whakatane, New Zealand
University of Dunedin, New Zealand, A.M., 1942
On staff Royal New Zealand Air Force, 1942-46
Knox Theological Hall, graduate, 1948
New College, Edinburgh University, Scotland, Ph.D., 1950
Union Theological Seminary, New York, 1951
Ordained Westchester Presbytery, 1951
Assistant Minister, Reformed Church, Bronxville, 1950-

MYERS, ALFRED EDWARD

b. New York, December 29, 1844
Williams College, 1866
New Brunswick Theological Seminary, 1866-67
Princeton Theological Seminary, 1868-69
Union Theological Seminary, 1869-70
Ordained October 9, 1870
Bethany Chapel, Brooklyn, N. Y., 1870-71
In Europe and Holy Land, 1871-72
Minister, Reformed Church, Bronxville, 1872-76
Minister, Presbyterian Church, Owasco, N. Y., 1877-85
Minister, Syracuse, N. Y., 1885-93
Assistant Minister, Marble Collegiate Church, New York, 1892-1915
Publications: *The Sociable, The Entertainment and the Bazaar, The Right Way of Giving*
d. September 16, 1915

POWELL, JOHN HENDERSON, JR.

b. Kansas City, Mo., October 19, 1898
Served with U. S. Naval Reserve, 1918
University of Illinois, A.B., 1920
Union Theological Seminary, Richmond, Va., B.D., 1925
Yale University, A.M., 1927
University of Edinburgh, Scotland, Ph.D., 1928
Olivet College, Olivet, Mich., D.D., 1949
Ordained Presbyterian Church, 1929
Assistant Pastor, St. Andrew's Church, Edinburgh, Scotland, 1927-28
Student Secretary Presbyterian Church, 1928-29
Representative, Reformed Church in America to 400th anniversary of the Reformation in Geneva, Switzerland, 1936
Representative, Reformed Church in America to 300th anniversary founding of University of Utrecht, 1936
Delegate to World Conference on Faith and Order, Edinburgh, 1937
Minister, Reformed Church, Bronxville, 1930-50
Publications: *How to Debate* (co-author), *The Ten Commandments*

RANKIN, JOHN JOSEPH

b. Newark, N. J., August 12, 1854
Williams College, 1876
Princeton Theological Seminary and Union Seminary, 1880
Licensed by Newark Presbytery, 1880
Ordained Buffalo Presbytery, 1883
Minister, Clarence, N. Y., 1883-85
Minister, Reformed Church, Bronxville, 1886-88

ROBERTSON, JAMES LOVEJOY

b. Steubenville, Ohio, September 5, 1837
Geneva College graduate, 1857. D.D., 1898
Allegheny Theological Seminary, 1859
Licensed by Steubenville Presbytery, 1857
Minister, Geneva, N. Y., 1859-67
Minister, Cincinnati, Ohio, 1867-70
Minister, Rochester, N. Y., 1870-77
Minister, Cleveland, Ohio, 1877-81
Minister, Cortland, N. Y., 1882-97
Minister, Galveston, Texas, 1897-99
Resident, Yonkers, N. Y., 1899-1903
Minister, Reformed Church, Bronxville, 1904-15
d. January 4, 1916

ROOSEVELT, WASHINGTON

b. Pelham, N. Y., 1802
Minister, Kinderhook, N. Y., 1846
Minister, Presbyterian Church, West 32nd Street, New York,
    1849-56
Minister, Reformed Church, Bronxville, 1857-72
d. February 11, 1884

RUNK, EDWARD JOHNSON

b. New York, N. Y., November 5, 1858
Columbia College, 1879
Union Theological Seminary, 1882
Ordained by Classis of Westchester, November 9, 1882
Minister, Reformed Church, Bronxville, 1882-84

SHAFFER, HOWARD CALVIN, JR.

b. Thomas, West Virginia, May 19, 1914
West Virginia University, A.B., 1935
Yale Divinity School, B.D., 1938
Ordained, Bronxville Reformed Church, June 18, 1939
Assistant Minister, Reformed Church, Bronxville, 1938-42
Minister, Colonial Church of Bayside (Reformed), Bayside, N. Y., 1942-

STEWART, ABEL T.

b. Somerville, N. J., August 4, 1822
Rutgers College, 1843; D.D., 1873
New Brunswick Theological Seminary, 1846
Licensed by Classis of New Brunswick
Minister, Greenville Reformed Church, 1846-50
Minister, Greenville and Bronxville Reformed Churches, 1850-52
Minister, First Reformed Church, Tarrytown, N. Y., 1852-55
Minister, Second Reformed Church, Holland, Mich., 1866-78
d. Watkins, N. Y., May 24, 1878

SWEET, LOUIS MATTHEWS

b. Southhold, N. Y., October 10, 1869
Hobart College, A.B., 1892; A.M., 1895; S.T.D., 1907
Auburn Theological Seminary graduate, 1895
New York University, Ph.D., 1918
Ordained Presbyterian ministry, 1895
Minister Presbyterian Churches at Union Springs, N. Y., Warsaw, N. Y., and Canandaigua, N. Y.
Professor Biblical Seminary, N. Y. and McCormick Theological Seminary, Chicago
Assistant Minister, Reformed Church, Bronxville, 1910-15
Stated Supply, Reformed Church, Bronxville, June 1915-February, 1916
Stated Supply, Reformed Church, Bronxville, spring and summer, 1919
Pulpit associate, Reformed Church, Bronxville, 1922-26
Frequent guest preacher, Reformed Church, Bronxville, July, 1929-January, 1930

WEBSTER, WILLIAM STUART CROSS

b. Baltimore, Md., September 12, 1844
College of New Jersey, 1864
Princeton University, 1869
Licensed by Classis of Luzerne, Pa.
Minister, Westerly, Pa., 1872-75; Port Jefferson, 1877-85; Islip, N. Y., 1885-97
Minister, Reformed Church, Bronxville, 1897-1903
d. Wayne, N. J., January 4, 1922

5

ELDERS

*James M. Prescott	1850-1860	H. Bertram Lewis	1930-1942
*James P. Swain	1850-1862	Myron G. Darby	1931-1939
*Caleb Smith	1852-1854	*Ferris J. Meigs	1932-1940
*Chipman Swain	1854-1857	Thomas B. Gilchrist	1933-
*Theodotus Burwell	1857-1889	Ralph W. Gwinn	1934-1945
*Alexander Masterton, Jr.		Harry Leslie Walker	1935-1946
	1861-1899	James Roberton MacColl, Jr	
*Alonzo Crittenden	1863-1864		1938-1948, 1951-
*Francis Bacon	1889-1902	*Raymond S. Crawford	1937-1943
*Frederick Sprenger	1900-1912	Jesse S. Phillips	1939-
*Frank R. Chambers	1902-1927	George F. Parton	1939-1949
*Elias W. Dusenberry		James E. Kavanagh	1939-1951
	1907-1916, 1927-1929	Charles B. Best	1942-1946
LaMont A. Warner	1912-1938	Henry Giebel	1942-1948, 1951-
*Benjamin E. Smythe	1912-1916	Harold M. Hess	1946-
*Charles Ruston	1916-1924	*William H. Webster	1946-1950
*Arthur C. Haff	1916-1927	Arthur F. Corwin	1946-
Burdette G. Lewis	1917-1918	Robcliff V. Jones	1945-1949
*Frank W. Wilson	1920-1929	Howard C. Sheperd	1948-
*Alan R. Fullarton	1921-1927	Frankland F. Stafford	1949-1951
*F. Bradley Reynolds	1924-1938	Neal T. McKee	1949-
*John J. Reigeluth	1927-1933	Arad Riggs	1950-
Dr. A. Livingston		Howard M. Erskine	1950-
Warnshuis	1927-1935	Francis B. Whitlock	1951-
*Edgar S. Bowling	1927-1950	Lewis V. Mays	1951-
*Donald M. Spaidal	1929-1932		

* Deceased

6

DEACONS

*Edward R. Hunt 1850-1853
*Alexander Masterton, Jr.
1850-1861
*James Turley 1852-1872-73
*Levi H. Crittenden 1853
*Dr. David E. Smith
1854-1862, 1866-1871
*Peter Shute 1854-1855
*Henry W. Crittenden 1863-1864
*James Ward 1864-1871
*Gilbert Shute 1872-1873
*Francis Bacon 1873-1889
*James C. Chambers 1874-1884
*Clarence Leggett 1880-1886
*Frederick Sprenger 1884-1899
*Samuel M. Stevenson 1887-1891
*Charles Dusenberry 1889-1895
*Alfred E. Smith, Jr. 1891-1911
*Jacob Egbert
1894-1912, 1913-1917
*W. P. H. Bacon 1896-1911
*Elias W. Dusenberry 1899-1907
William B. Jennings 1908-1909
*Benjamin E. Smythe 1910-1912
Lemuel A. Welles 1911-1917
Thomas W. Harris 1911-1913
*Almon C. Barrell 1912-1916
Harry D. Nims 1912-1916
*Hugh S. Robertson
1916-1918, 1927-1929
Harry Leslie Walker 1916-1918
Ralph W. Gwinn 1917-1919,
1927-1929, 1931-1933
Charles B. Best 1917-1919
*A. C. G. Hammesfahr
1918-1919, 1920-1922
John E. Roeser 1918-1920

*Dr. Brainerd H. Whitbeck
1919-1921
Russell C. Jones 1919-1921
Howard S. F. Randolph
1920-1922
George H. Beach 1920
Harry E. Pollard 1921-1924
David Lamb 1921-1923
William O. Packard 1921-1923
Joseph H. Clark 1921-1923
Thomas B. Gilchrist
1922-1924, 1930-1932
*F. Bradley Reynolds 1922-1924
John E. S. Barker 1923-1925
Rolland J. Hamilton
1923-1926, 1929-1931
*Walter A. Shaw 1923-1925, 1927
Russell K. Boadwee 1924
Spencer T. Horton 1924-1926
*Donald M. Spaidal 1924-1926
*Edgar S. Bowling 1925-1927
David C. Coyle 1925-1927
Robcliff V. Jones
1925-1927, 1930-1932
Myron G. Darby 1926-1928
*Charles Steele 1926-1928
*Ferris J. Meigs 1926-1928
Clinton C. Swan
1927-1929, 1934-1936
Jesse S. Phillips 1928-1930
R. Hunter McQuistion 1928-1930
H. Bertram Lewis 1928-1930
George F. Parton 1929-1931
Lindsay H. Crawford 1929-1931
Harold M. Hess 1930-1932
*William L. Colt 1930-1932
*Raymond S. Crawford 1931-1933

* Deceased

168

Howard M. Erskine	1931-1933	William J. Cunningham	
Luther G. McConnell	1931-1933		1943-1947
William E. Tucker	1932-1934	Alexander Hadden	1944-1948
Howard V. Smith	1932-1934	Lewis V. Mays	1944-1948
Henry W. Doyle	1933-1937	Frankland F. Stafford	1944-1948
James Roberton MacColl, Jr.		Blevins C. Dunklin	1945-1949
	1933-1937	Jay E. Mason	1945-1947
D. Porter Hughes	1934-1938	Arad Riggs	1945-1949
Romney L. Campbell	1935-1939	Albert H. Hardenbergh	
Henry Giebel	1935-1939		1945-1949
Chester Wiese	1936-1939	F. Wilson Keller	1946-1950
O. Dickinson Street		Joseph T. Mirtl	1946-1950
	1936-1940, 1941-1945	Kenneth K. Stowell	1946-1948
Arthur F. Corwin	1936-1940	McGregor Demarest	1947-1950
George A. Jacoby	1937-1941	Frank L. Dewey	1947-1950
William Cook	1937-1941	Harry M. Rounds	1947-1951
Frederick H. Bair	1938-1942	Joel Hunter, Jr.	1948-
Leland Rex Robinson	1939-1943	James Reynolds	1948-1949
Francis B. Whitlock	1939-1943	Paul E. Tobin	1948-
*William H. Webster	1939-1943	Richard W. Ince	1949-
*Henry H. Cone, Jr.		Lee M. Fuller	1949-
	1940-1942, 1948-1950	Dr. John Ross	1949-
William C. Stowell	1940-1944	Hubert A. Howson	1949-
*Karl D. Gardner	1941-1943	Henry C. L. Johnson	1950-
*Frederick W. Edmondson		William Macfarlane	1950-
	1942-1944	John L. Carson	1950-
Richard D. Hillis	1942-1946	Charles B. Lauren	1950-
E. A. Baily	1943-1947	Edmund B. Boynton	1951-
John P. Holmes	1943-1947	J. W. Cunningham	1951-
D. Frank Webster	1943-1947		

7

CLERKS OF CONSISTORY

*Alexander Masterton, Jr.		George A. Jacoby	1938-1941
	1850-1899	Francis B. Whitlock	1941-1943
*Frederick Sprenger	1899-1912	Richard D. Hillis	1943-1946
*Elias W. Dusenberry	1912-1916	Blevins C. Dunklin	1946-1948
*Charles Ruston	1916-1924	Frank L. Dewey	1948-1949
LaMont A. Warner	1924-1938	Hubert A. Howson	1949-

* Deceased

169

8

TREASURERS OF THE CHURCH

*Alexander Masterton, Jr.		Howard S.F.Randolph	1921-1923
	1850-1873	John E. Roeser	1923-1925
*Francis Bacon	1873-1891	*Frank Dinsmore	1925-1946
*Frederick Sprenger	1891-1895	Lewis V. Mays	1946-1948
*Jacob Egbert	1895-1921	Joel Hunter, Jr.	1948-

9

DIRECTORS OF RELIGIOUS EDUCATION AND SUPERINTENDENTS OF THE CHURCH SCHOOL

James Minot Prescott	1850-1874	Superintendent
Alexander Masterton, Jr.	1874-1899	Superintendent
Frank R. Chambers	1899-1921	Superintendent
	1921-1939	Superintendent, Emeritus
LaMont A. Warner	1919-1921	Assistant Superintendent
James Coffin Stout	1920-1927	Superintendent
William Thomas Heath	1926-1929	Assistant Minister — Superintendent
Frederick L. Fay	1928-1933	Director of Religious Education
William McCance	1933-1938	Assistant Minister — Superintendent
Howard C. Shaffer	1938-1942	Assistant Minister — Superintendent
Mrs. O. J. Gette	1942-	Director of Religious Education
George A. Ackerly	1945-1949	Associate Minister — Teacher
Ronald William McNeur	1950-	Assistant Minister

* Deceased

10

PRESIDENTS OF THE WOMEN'S SOCIETY

Mrs. Barrett Andrews 1912-1914
Mrs. Harry D. Nims 1914-1915
*Mrs. Joseph H. Beall 1915-1917
Mrs. Harry Leslie Walker
                           1917-1919
Mrs. Ferris J. Meigs 1919-1921
Mrs. Charles W. Halsey
                           1921-1922
Mrs. F. Bradley Reynolds
                           1922-1924
Mrs. Ferris J. Meigs 1924-1927
Mrs. Ralph H. Stearns 1927-1929
Mrs. Raymond S. Crawford
                           1929-1931
Miss Katherine T. Halsey
                           1931-1933

Mrs. James A. Farrell 1933-1935
Miss Elizabeth T. Wilson
                           1935-1937
Mrs. William L. Colt 1937-1939
Mrs. Harold M. Hess 1939-1941
Mrs. Ralph W. Gwinn 1941-1943
Mrs. Kenneth K. Stowell
                           1943-1945
Mrs. F. Wilson Keller 1945-1947
Mrs. Neal Trimble McKee
                           1947-1949
Mrs. Francis B. Whitlock
                           1949-1951
Mrs. Jackson Chambers
                           1951-

11

PRESIDENTS OF THE MEN'S CLUB

Rolland J. Hamilton
Thomas B. Gilchrist
Myron G. Darby
A. C. G. Hammesfahr

Clinton C. Swan
George F. Parton
Henry P. Warren

After Reorganization

George F. Parton
Henry W. Doyle
William J. Cunningham
Howard M. Erskine

Frankland F. Stafford
George H. Elliott
Albert H. Hardenbergh
Paul E. Tobin

* Deceased

12

1929-30 COMMITTEE FOR THE SELECTION OF A MINISTER TO SUCCEED THE REVEREND DEANE EDWARDS

A. L. Warnshuis, *Chairman*

W. P. H. Bacon
J. E. S. Barker
Mrs. Charles Francis Bates
Edgar S. Bowling
William L. Colt
Lindsay H. Crawford
Mrs. Raymond S. Crawford
Myron G. Darby
Frank Dinsmore
Miss Amie S. Dusenberry
Mrs. O. J. Gette
Thomas B. Gilchrist
Ralph W. Gwinn
Mrs. Charles W. Halsey
Rolland J. Hamilton
A. C. G. Hammesfahr
Harold M. Hess
H. Bertram Lewis

R. Hunter McQuistion
Ferris J. Meigs
Harry D. Nims
George F. Parton
Jesse S. Phillips
E. E. Quantrell
Donald Reigeluth
John J. Reigeluth
F. B. Reynolds
Miss Nell Russell
Howard V. Smith
Donald M. Spaidal
Clinton C. Swan
Stephen A. Van Ness
LaMont A. Warner
Frank W. Wilson
Roger A. Young

13

1949-50 COMMITTEE FOR THE SELECTION OF A MINISTER TO SUCCEED DR. JOHN HENDERSON POWELL, JR.

Thomas B. Gilchrist, *Chairman*; Arad Riggs, *Vice-Chairman*; Mrs. Helen Powers Revellese, *Secretary-Clerk*

Mrs. John L. Carson
Mrs. Jackson Chambers
Mrs. Donald K. Clifford
Myron G. Darby
Charles Doerr
Edward K. Fiencke
Lee M. Fuller

Paul L. Geiringer
Albert H. Hardenbergh
Harold M. Hess
John P. Holmes
Richard W. Ince
Henry C. L. Johnson
Mrs. F. Wilson Keller

172

Charles B. Lauren
James Roberton MacColl, Jr.
William Macfarlane
Mrs. Russell McCandless
Mrs. Neal T. McKee
George F. Parton
Leland R. Robinson

Floyd S. Sanford
O. Dickinson Street
Mrs. Harry Leslie Walker
Mrs. Francis B. Whitlock
Miss Helen B. Wilson
Mrs. Daniel E. Woodhull, Jr.

14

NAMES ON MARBLE SLAB IN CHURCH FLOOR NEAR PULPIT

1868	Mary H. Blackmire	1864	George Kimbler
	Infant of William Booth	1869	Paul Pope
1857	Jesse Bottomley	1872	John Maasley
1862	Maria Bottomley		James Seymour
1863	Charles Boyd	1875	Infant of D. Pearsall
1860	George Boyd	1868	Infant of J. Pearsall
1863	Mrs. George Boyd	1864	William Spooner
1860	Walter Boyd		Child of F. Lemtern
	Infant of J. Cilkendar		Mrs. Sherwood
	Mrs. John Corbage		Son of Wm. Scott
	Child of John Corbage	1865	William
1900	Frederick Elliott	1886	Susan Stuart
1872	Infant of F. Elliott	1860	Frederick Ward
1878	Jennie Elliott		Infant of J. Ward
1883	Margaret Elliott	1900	Annie Wilson
1862	Infant of Evans Evans	1864	Thos. A. Wilson
	Infant of Samuel Fee		Mrs. T. A. Wilson
1872	John Gabie	1862	Child of James Shipman
1863	Mrs. John Gabie	1864	Jennie Steibeling
1861	Mary Johnson	1865	Margaret Steibeling
1860	Infant of William Hague		Mrs. Wilder
	Infant of A. Inkleman		Andrew Kenifick
1861	Sarah Hargraves		Mrs. Andrew Kenifick
1873	Infant of Chas. Kearnes	1866	Wm. H. Wilson
1878	Infant of H. Turley	1877	Fletcher Wilson
1865	Frederick Streck	1887	W. H. Wilson

15

NAMES ON BRONZE TABLET
WORLD WAR I

Timothy F. Allen, Jr.
Thomas P. Allenby
James A. Allister
Hannah D. Andrews
Joseph H. Clark
Morris S. Clark
Harold D. Cooper
Elmer M. Ellsworth
Frank Ferris
Arthur N. Ferris
William C. Fisher
Christian G. Franzius
Ernest H. Geyer
Linwood H. Geyer
Charles W. Halsey
C. Henry Hathaway
Clara M. Heimerle
Harry Heimerle
Raymond K. Howe
Donald A. Howe

Lewis S. Latimer
Alfred T. Latimer
William J. McIntyre
Winter Mead
Henry C. Merritt, Jr.
Schuyler Merritt 2nd
Harold H. Mueller
Felix E. Mueller
Carl J. Nim
Harry D. Nims
Frederick C. Payne
William J. Robb, Jr.
Herbert J. Schwader
Frederick R. Spencer
Penrose V. Stout
Robert W. Tait
William O. Tait, Jr.
Nathan Tufts
Richard A. Weisfelder
Brainerd H. Whitbeck

16

NAMES ON THE ROLL OF HONOR
WORLD WAR II

William C. Abbe
Albert E. Abendschein
George Akerson
John S. Allard
Philip G. Alston
William Henry Alston, Jr.
William Watson Alston
Crawford Earle Appleman
Martin Sybial Arbonies
Christian H. Armbruster

John Worth Armbruster
Raymond T. Armbruster
Edward A. Baily, Jr.
Barbara R. Bair
Eldridge Bair
Frederick H. Bair, Jr.
Lawrence W. Baker
David C. Barker
Wilson F. Barnes, Jr.
Peter N. Barr

Robert T. Barr
Thomas Barr
Almon Colburn Barrell
Halsey V. Barrett
Robert H. Barrows
David Bartlett
Edward R. Bartlett, Jr.
Mansfield M. Bascom
Roger W. Bates
Charles H. Bechtold
Herbert W. Bennett
Curtis Berrien
Price Berrien
A. Jefferson Berry
Edith A. Manzer Bickford
Arthur W. Biddle
Harry A. Biddle
Herbert Biddle
John N. Biddle
John Bidwell
Edward L. Bishop, Jr.
Philip J. Bliss
Berry Bonynge
Russell Bonynge
Russell Bonynge, Jr.
Henry Robert Booth
Wayland R. Bourne
Clyde S. Bouton
Clyde S. Bouton, Jr.
Milton S. Bowman
Robert G. Bowman
*Roger G. B. Broome, III
Bailey Warren Brown
Charles Hinkle Brown
Robert Duncan Brown, Jr.
Wm. P. J. Brunet de Rochebrune
C. Clark Bryan
Milton Burton
*Helene Wack Burnett

Layard Campbell
William G. Campbell
Hugh C. Campfield
John L. Carson
Clara Frances Clapp
E. Gardner Clapp
Bradford Clark
Carl Alton Clark
Sears Yates Coker
Charles William Coldwell
Robert Coldwell
Frank C. Cole, Jr.
Robert Lloyd Cole
Mortimer Barkley Coley
Henry Houghton Cone, Jr.
Frank Gideon Cooley, III
Edwin Hawley Crandell
John U. Crandell
Walter Bain Crandell
William S. Crompton
Louis P. Davis
Rex Deane
Paul DeMagnin
Peter A. DeMott
Raymond S. DeMott
Elizabeth Clark Devereux
Morse Grant Dial, Jr.
Frederick N. Dibble
Harold E. Djorup
Arthur R. Dornheim
Henry Watkins Doyle, Jr.
Roy D. Duckworth, Jr.
Clifford H. Dwinnell
Houston Eagle
Edwin H. Eaton
Frederick W. Edmondson, Jr.
Thomas C. Edwards, Jr.
Donald L. Elliman
Douglas Elliott

* Gold Star

Farnsworth Elliott
Basil B. Elmer
Basil B. Elmer, Jr.
Colby R. Esterbrook
William H. Fairweather, M.D.
MacLennan Farrell
Nancy Farrell
Lawrence Ferling
*Richard Hunter Field
John Gene Flack
Julius Vincent Flack, M.D.
Anson J. Fowler, II
Frederick M. Fradley
John Berry Francis
Edward A. Gage, II
Herbert N. Gardner
*Karl D. Gardner
William Gardner
Sprague G. Garlock
Theodore Ross Gates
Francis Thomas Gephart
Carlton R. Gette
John O. Gette, Jr.
Harry W. Getting, Jr.
Robert R. Giebel
Thomas B. Gilchrist, Jr.
Melville K. Gill
Arthur Tomlin Goodman, Jr.
Nancy Erskine Grace
Lindsay Grant
Henry E. Greene
Lewis S. Griffith
Dana Gumb
Irving T. Gumb, Jr.
Robert L. Gwinn
Richard C. Hall
William J. Harper, Jr.
John S. Hathaway
Russell Henderson
Roger S. Henry

Robert K. Hess
H. Edward Hildebrand, Jr.
Nancy Hillis
Edward D. Hinton
Edward Franklin Hitch
C. Whitman Hobbs, III
Powell W. Holbein
J. Thomas Holbrook, Jr.
Samuel T. Hubbard, III
Thomas B. Hubbard
William H. Hubbard, II
Harold G. Hubbel, Jr.
Blake Hughes
Richard W. Ince
John Inman
Robert Inman
George W. Jack
Jane Anne McKee Jack
Henry C. L. Johnson
Paul Johnson
*Robert A. Johnson
James Monroe Jones, M.D.
Robcliff V. Jones, Jr.
Sandy Kahn
Karl A. Kaiser
John H. Kavanagh
John Kent
Byron B. Kenyon, M.D.
Colin R. Kidd
Irving H. Kingman
Donald Kivell
Kenneth E. Kleine
R. Leland Knowles, Jr.
Lester A. Lake, Jr.
Frederick L. Landau, M.D.
John Landenberger
Fleetwood Lanneau
Lewis S. Latimer
Michael W. Lau
Marshall H. Leckner

Arthur V. Lee, III
Richard L. Leeds
Paul Damon Littlefield
Cynthia Lowrey
Lawson G. Lowrey
Richard S. Lowrey
Gifford W. Mabie
E. Kimbark MacColl
James Roberton MacColl, III
David Mackintosh
William Mackintosh, Jr.
Ward N. Madison
*Richard Robinson Major
*Clifford M. Markle
Gordon M. Markle, II
Joseph Mason
Richard L. Matthews
William C. Matthews
Albert T. Maurice
L. Victor Mays
Alan McBride
Edward Archer McBride
Russell McCandless
Thomas R. McCleary
William Kenneth McCleary
David Graham McConnell
Graham Slagle McConnell, M.D.
John Stuart McConnell
Victor C. McCutcheon
Edwin C. McDonald, Jr.
Chester B. McLaughlin, Jr.
John Norris McLean
Donald Hunter McQuistion
George Nichol McVicar
Walter Dodge McVicar
Arthur W. Miller
Robert Ellis Miller, Jr.
Robert H. Miller
Donald R. Moffett, Jr.
John K. Moffett

William Moffett
David Channing Moore
William J. Morden
Charles Gill Morgan
Edwin H. Morse
David W. Morton, Jr.
Robert Creech Myers
John H. Naylor, Jr.
George F. Neiley, Jr.
Marion E. Newson
George Guernsey Nichols, Jr.
Marshall G. Nims
Robert G. Nims
Anne G. Nims Nixon
Arnold Nye
Richard Edgar O'Daniel
Arthur H. Oesterheld, Jr.
Edwin H. Oesterheld
Hamilton O'Hara
*Robert R. O'Loughlin, Jr.
Charles William Parton
George F. Parton, Jr.
Howard Patterson
David Markham Patton
Paul L. Peyton, Jr.
Knox B. Phagan
Knox B. Phagan, Jr.
Joseph C. Pickard
Wallace F. Pickard
Harvey K. Pinger
Morgan Pirnie
James W. Poe, Jr.
David Taylor Pontius
Robert M. Prentice
James Donald Quale
Morton Quantrell
*Edward E. Quimby
Wallace L. Quimby
Amy Lou Cowing Redfield
Howard L. Rees

Kenneth Rees
James P. Rich
Daniel H. Robbins
Frederick C. Robbins
William C. Robbins
John M. Roeser
Conrad Roney
Donald S. Root
E. Edgar Routh, Jr.
John W. Routh
W. Nelson Routh
Philip Winthrop Russell
Alvin R. Safford
Alfred L. Sauter
*Carl W. Sautter
Robert Underwood Sautter
Robert Schaaf
Pierre Schiltz
John William Schmalz, Jr.
David J. Scott
Howard Scott
James T. Seaver, Jr.
George Seybolt
William H. Shailer
David Sherrick
*Howard Cotterill Sheperd, Jr.
Eugene E. Sitterley
John T. Skinner
Louis E. Skinner, Jr.
Hartley Perry Smith
Howard V. Smith, Jr.
Mason Smith
William Armstrong Smith, Jr.
Frank W. Spencer, Jr.
Joseph M. Spencer
Gordon C. Stenhouse
Arnold Steuhl
Arthur Steuhl
Fred J. Steuhl
Harry E. Steuhl

John K. M. Stevens
William H. Stevens
John Wesley Stewart
Chandler D. Stone
George J. Stork
*Bruce Kingsley Stowell
O. Dickinson Street, Jr.
Charles A. Sweet, Jr.
Robert R. Sweet
Robert Edward Syska
Colin Tyson Taylor
Gardner W. Taylor, II
Bartholomew G. Tenore
George Lyman Tenore
Maurice J. Terman
John H. Thoerner
*Loring Thompson
Roderick G. Thompson
Roger W. Thompson
*Charles A. Tier
Edgar S. Tilton, Jr.
James Russell Tippett
Willoughby Todd
Richard Trapp
*J. Carter Treadwell
Bruce Pearson Van Buskirk
David Van Buskirk
*Douglas Byrd Van Buskirk
Eliot N. Vestner
Leroy B. Voshall
James Warden
David A. Warren
Lincoln F. Warren
Harry F. Washburn, Jr.
Howard Wilfred Watts
Leslie F. Weaver
* A. Mangum Webb
David Kenyon Webster
Frank Josiah Webster
George Morgan Webster

178

John K. O. Webster
Jacob Frederick Weintz
James W. Weston
Richard P. Wheeler
Lawrence W. Whitaker
Franklin P. Whitbeck
Paul Grant Williams, Jr.
Frederick Wilson

*Robert P. Wilson
William H. Wilterdink
Arthur Wingebach
Walter G. Winslow
Daniel E. Woodhull, Jr.
Roy Donald Wooster, Jr.
James Worth
Roger Young

17

NAMES OF THE CONTRIBUTORS TO THE WAR MEMORIAL WINDOW FUND

Abbe, Mrs. William
Abbe, Frances
Achilles, Mr. and Mrs. Paul S.
Achilles, Constance
Achilles, Nancy
Alden, John P. C.
Allard, Mrs. John S.
Allen, Claud
Allen, Julia S.
Allen, Mr. and Mrs. Timothy F.
Ames, Charles Hayden
Ames, Woodward W.
Anderson, Mrs. Jean Frame
Arbonies, Lt. and Mrs. Martin S.
Armbruster, Dorothy M.
Armbruster, Marion H.
Armstrong, Mrs. Emily S.
Ashby, Mr. and Mrs. Aubrey L.
Ashby, Marjorie Lee
Ashton, Mr. and Mrs. Henry R.
Bacon, Mrs. William P. H.
Baily, Mr. and Mrs. Edward A.
Baily, Edward A., Jr.
Baily, Frederick G.
Baker, Mr. and Mrs. Harold W.
Ball, Mr. and Mrs. Raymond C.
Ball, Barbara M.

Barker, Mr. and Mrs. J. E. S.
Barker, Janice Lee
Barker, Lawrence David
Barker, Lynn Ann
Barker, Wendy Ann
Barnard, T. Winthrop
Barnard, Mr. and Mrs.
  Winthrop F.
Barnard, Mary Boots
Barr, Mr. and Mrs. Joseph R.
Barr, Robert J.
Barr, Thomas A.
Bascom, Mrs. Pearle Boyd
Bates, Col. and Mrs.
  Charles Francis
Bates, Frances White
Bechtold, Dr. and Mrs. A. C.
Bechtold, Charles Harrison
Berry, Mrs. Andrew J., Jr.
Best, Mr. and Mrs. Charles B.
Biddle, Mrs. Louise K.
Biddle, Beatrice K.
Biddle, Virginia Ruth
Biddle, Arthur W.
Biddle, Herbert F.
Bidwell, Mrs. John
Bishop, Mrs. Edward L.

Bisland, Mr. and Mrs. Pressley E.
Bixler, Mr. and Mrs. David D.
Bixler, David D., Jr.
Bixler, Freeman
Bliss, Mr. and Mrs. Julius
Bliss, Donald R.
Bliss, Philip J.
Blodgett, Mrs. Eleanor Clark
Blomberg, Mr. and Mrs.
   August M.
Blomberg, Martha Ann
Bogie, Betty Lou
Bogie, Marjorie D.
Bogie, Mord, III
Booth, Mr. and Mrs. Henry
Booth, Henry Robert
Booth, Nancy Lane
Booth, Virginia Elizabeth
Borgeson, Dr. and Mrs. Frithiof C.
Borgeson, Roger D.
Borgeson, Ruth D.
Bouton, Dr. and Mrs. Clyde S.
Bouton, Clyde S., Jr.
Bouton, William C.
Bowling, Mr. and Mrs. Edgar S.
Bowman, Mrs. M. S.
Boynton, Mrs. George M.
Brebner, Elliott
Brinsmade, Mr. and Mrs.
   Hobart L.
Brinsmade, Louis
Brinsmade, Sara Lee
Brown, Lt. and Mrs.
   Bailey Warren
Brown, Bailey Warren, Jr.
Brown, Lt. and Mrs. Charles H.
Brown, Mrs. Harry Whiting, Sr.
Brown, Mr. and Mrs. Harry W.
Brown, Mr. and Mrs.
   Thomas Morgan

Brunet de Rochebrune,
   Mrs. W. P. J.
Brunet de Rochebrune, Frank C.
Brunet de Rochebrune, Johanna G.
Brunet de Rochebrune, Theodore J.
Bryant, Mr. and Mrs. Carl C.
Bryant, Caroline S.
Bryant, Sandra C.
Buell, Edith M.
Buell, Walter H.
Calkins, Rose Mary
Cameron, Mr. and Mrs. William D.
Campbell, Mr. and Mrs.
   Romney L.
Campbell, Virginia
Chambers, Mrs. Frank R.
Chapman, Mr. and Mrs. Alger B.
Chapman, Alger B., Jr.
Chapman, Carol
Chapman, Hilda I.
Chapman, William C.
Clark, Mr. and Mrs. Chester M.
Clifford, Mr. and Mrs. Donald K.
Clifford, Donald K., Jr.
Clifford, Louise M.
Clifford, Margery M., Jr.
Cochrane, Mrs. Samuel Bruce
Coker, Major and Mrs. S. Yates
Coldwell, Mr. and Mrs. Everett S.
Coldwell, Robert S.
Coldwell, C. William
Cole, Mrs. Helen Lloyd and family
Cole, Lois Gregory
Cole, Mrs. M. Cochrane
Cole, Lt. and Mrs. Philip G., Jr.
Coley, Mrs. Mortimer B.
Cone, Mrs. Henry H., Jr.
Cook, William and family
Copeland, Jane N.
Corbus, Mr. and Mrs. Edward T.

Corwin, Arthur F.
Coulton, Mr. and Mrs. John M.
Crandell, Mrs. Walter S.
Crawford, Homer
Crawford, Mr. and Mrs. R. S.
Crompton, Lynne McKean
Cumming, Mr. and Mrs. Robert B.
Cunningham, Ann
Cunningham, Richard
Cunningham, Mr. and Mrs.
    William J.
Curtis, Anne
Curtis, Mr. and Mrs. Edward G.
Curtis, Edward M.
Curtis, Eleanor
Curtis, Helen Virginia
Curtis, Mr. and Mrs. John Avery
Curtis, Katherine Edna
Curtis, Mary Gilman
Darby, Mr. and Mrs. Myron G.
Darby, Mary
Darby, Myron G., Jr.
Dargan, Mrs. J. F., Jr.
Davies, Dr. and Mrs. Joshua W.
Davies, Joshua W., Jr.
Davies, Ruth Kinser
Davis, Mr. and Mrs. Lawrence A.
Deane, Joan E.
Deane, Margaret M.
Deane, Nancy M.
DeLong, Mrs. Dorothy Hobbs
DeLong, Charles F.
Demarest, Mr. and Mrs. L. M.
Demmon, Mr. and Mrs. Roy Earl
Demmon, Roy E., Jr.
DeMott, Lucien Keith
DeMott, Peter A.
DeMott, Mrs. Raymond S.
DePaul, Hazel
DePaul, Neil

DePaul, Philip
Deverman, Mr. and Mrs.
    Charles E.
Dewey, Mr. and Mrs. Frank
Dial, Mr. and Mrs. Morse G.
Dietz, Mr. and Mrs. Ernest C. W.
Dietz, Jessie Reid
Dinsmore, Frank
Djorup, Mrs. Olga
Djorup, Richard C.
Dornheim, Betty M.
Dornheim, Mr. and Mrs. G. A.
Douglas, Mr. and Mrs. Arthur
Dreyer, Mrs. Marie E.
Dudley, Anne G.
Dudley, Dorothy W.
Dudley, Henry Lewis, Jr.
Dunklin, Anne P.
Dunklin, Mr. and Mrs. Blevins C.
Dunklin, Blevins C., Jr.
Dusenberry, Elias W.
Dwinell, Lt. Clifford H.
Dwinell, Mrs. E. H.
Dwinell, Malvin E.
Dwinell, Raymond M.
Eaton, Mr. and Mrs. Edward A.
Eddy, Mr. and Mrs. George A.
Eddy, Jonathan E. B.
Edmondson, Mr. and Mrs. F. W.
Edmondson, Eleanor
Elliott, Mr. and Mrs. A. H.
Elliott, Farnsworth
Elliott, Sydney
Emmel, Alfred C. and family
Erskine, Carol W.
Erskine, Mr. and Mrs. Howard M.
Erskine, Howard W.
Farrell, Mr. and Mrs. James A.
Farrell, Mrs. J. Fletcher
Farrell, MacLennan

Farrell, Nancy
Ferris, Mr. and Mrs. Arthur N.
Ferris, Frances Louise
Ferris, Frank
Ferris, Marie Louise
Ferris, Sue Ann
Ferris, Mrs. William Nelson
Field, Mr. and Mrs. J. Hunter
Finch, Mr. and Mrs. Charles A.
Fisher, Bradford
Fisher, Mr. and Mrs. H. Earl
Fisher, Sally
Flack, Mr. and Mrs. Eugene W.
Ford, Barbara
Ford, Mr. and Mrs. Donald
Ford, Donald, Jr.
Foster, Mr. and Mrs. Richard W.
Foster, Richard W., Jr.
Fox, Jane Bleecker
Fox, Kathryn Auger, Jr.
Fox, Mr. and Mrs. Noel Bleecker
Fox, Norman
Franzius, Mr. and Mrs.
   Christian G.
Fraser, Annie G.
Friberg, Mr. and Mrs. Andrew
Frost, Arthur Corwin
Frost, Claudia Elizabeth
Frost, Mr. and Mrs.
   Frederick G., Jr.
Frost, Frederick G., III
Gardner, Mr. and Mrs. Karl D.
Gardner, William J.
Gardner, Katherine E.
Garlock, Eleanor M.
Garlock, Mr. and Mrs. Morgan B.
Garlock, Roger B.
Garlock, Lt. Sprague G.
Genung, Mrs. Merwin E.
Genung, Muriel E.

Gette, Mr. and Mrs. John Otto
Gibson, Mr. and Mrs. C. R.
Giebel, Mr. and Mrs. Henry
Giebel, Robert R.
Gilbert, Mr. and Mrs. Maurice E.
Gilbert, Maurice E., Jr.
Gilchrist, Gail
Gilchrist, Juliet G.
Gilchrist, Mr. and Mrs. Thomas B.
Good, Mrs. James W.
Goodman, Mr. and Mrs. Arthur T.
Goodman, Arthur T., Jr.
Goodman, Julie R.
Grace, Mrs. Nancy Erskine
Grafius, Andrew B.
Grant, Mr. and Mrs. Lindsay
Gray, Mrs. Eva K.
Gray, Mrs. Harriet A.
Greene, Mr. and Mrs. Henry E.
Greene, Henry E., Jr.
Gudos, Mrs. Peter
Guerdan, Mr. and Mrs. George A.
Guerdan, Constance R.
Guerdan, David G.
Guerdan, Roderick A.
Gwinn, Mr. and Mrs. David M.
Gwinn, Eleanor E.
Gwinn, Mr. and Mrs. Gordon T.
Gwinn, John Charles
Gwinn, Nancy V.
Gwinn, Mr. and Mrs. Ralph W.
Gwinn, Richard
Hadden, Mr. and Mrs. Alexander
Hadden, Alexander, Jr.
Hadden, Edith B.
Hadden, Robert W.
Halsey, Katherine T.
Hardenbergh, Mr. and Mrs.
   Henry
Hardenbergh, Lois N.

Haskell, Mr. and Mrs. William P.
Hathaway, Mr. and Mrs.
   C. Henry
Hathaway, John S.
Hawks, Mrs. Marion Jones
Hegeman, Bertram
Heimerle, Clara M.
Henderson, Dr. and Mrs. A. B.
Henderson, Carol
Henderson, Helen
Henderson, Mr. and Mrs. Howard
Henderson, Howard Russell
Henderson, Susan
Henderson, Sylvia
Hendricks, Mr. and Mrs.
   W. Homer
Hendrickson, Eva Tredwell
Henry, Mrs. Elizabeth Barr
Henry, Peter Barr
Herbold, Mr. and Mrs. Edward
Hess, Mr. and Mrs. Harold M.
Hess, Lt. Robert Kellogg
Hillis, Anne R.
Hillis, Elizabeth R.
Hillis, Margaret R.
Hillis, Nancy R.
Hillis, Mr. and Mrs. Richard D.
Hinton, Mrs. Edgar D.
Hobbs, Mr. and Mrs. Clarence W.
Hobbs, C. Whitman, Jr.
Holbein, Anne Rosseau
Holbein, Mr. and Mrs. Edgar A.
Holbein, Powell W.
Holmes, Mr. and Mrs. John P.
Holmes, John P., Jr.
Holmes, Pattie P.
Holmes, Russell P.
Houghton, Helen
Houghton, Margaret T.
Houghton, Mr. and Mrs. V. T.

Howell, Eva
Howell, Lillian C.
Howson, Mr. and Mrs. Hubert A.
Howson, Hubert Farnham
Howson, John Abbe
Hubbard, Mr. and Mrs. S. T., Jr.
Hubbard, Captain S. T., III
Hubbard, Lt. and Mrs. Thomas B.
Hubbard, William H., II
Hulsapple, Lesley Carol
Hulsapple, Mr. and Mrs. M. B.
Ince, Mrs. Martha Good
Jack, Mr. and Mrs.
   George Wilfred
Jayme, Mrs. J. Philip
Jayme, Phyllis
Johnson, Mrs. Henry C. L.
Johnson, Frederick A.
Jones, Mr. and Mrs. H. Lloyd
Jones, Mary Isabel
Jones, Mr. and Mrs. Robcliff V.
Jones, Robcliff V., Jr.
Karlen, Mrs. Catherine Booth
Kavanagh, Mr. and Mrs. James E.
Kavanagh, Mrs. Jessamine H.
Keller, Marilyn Marie
Kent, Mrs. Margaret Ley
Kent, John E.
Kingman, Mr. and Mrs. Samuel E.
Kivell, Mr. and Mrs. Wayne A.
Kivell, Donald W.
Kurtz, Mr. and Mrs. Francis M.
Kurtz, F. Mason
Kurtz, Richard C.
Lake, Mr. and Mrs. Lester A.
Landenberger, Mrs. O. A.
Lang, Alfred H.
Lang, Marie Alice
Lang, Winifred
Lawrence, Mr. and Mrs. John F.

Lee, Mr. and Mrs. Arthur V., Jr.
Lee, Mrs. Harry M.
Lee, Betty
Leeds, Linda
Leeds, Mrs. Mary L. Gilchrist
Leininger, Mr. and Mrs. A. R.
Leininger, Nancy B.
Levino, Joan
Lewis, Mr. and Mrs. H. Bertram
Littlefield, Lt. j.g. and Mrs. P. D.
Lobenstein, Mrs. James C.
Lonkay, Mr. and Mrs. L. T.
Lonkay, Kitty
Mabie, Mr. and Mrs. Gifford M.
Mabie, Gifford M., Jr.
Mabie, Gordon W.
Mabie, Mr. and Mrs. Edmund G.
Mabie, William B.
MacColl, E. Kimbark
MacColl, Mr. and Mrs.
   J. Roberton, Jr.
MacColl, Rev. and Mrs.
   J. Roberton, III
Mackay, Marguerite
Mackintosh, David
Mackintosh, Mrs. William
Mackintosh, Lt. j.g. and Mrs.
   Wm., Jr.
Mann, Mr. and Mrs. A. R.
Markle, Mrs. Clifford M.
Markle, Elizabeth Louise
Markle, Gordon Mears, II
Marsh, Mr. and Mrs. Reginald E.
Mason, Mr. and Mrs. Jay E.
Maxson, Mr. and Mrs.
   L. Meredith
Mays, Mr. and Mrs. Lewis V.
Mays, Lewis V., Jr.
McCleary, Bill
McCleary, Dorothy

McCleary, Joan
McCleary, Mr. and Mrs. T. R.
McCleary, Tom
McConnell, Mrs. Graham Slagle
McConnell, Helen
McConnell, Mr. and Mrs.
   Luther G.
McConnell, Mary
McConnell, Sara Lee
McDonald, James G.
McKee, Mr. and Mrs.
   Neal Trimble
McMillan, Mrs. Mary MacColl
McQuistion, Mr. and Mrs.
   R. Hunter
Mead, Jennie E.
Mead, Louise A.
Mead, Nellie L.
Meade, Mr. and Mrs. Frank D.
Mellis, Margery
Merchant, Mr. and Mrs. Ely O.
Merchant, Ely O., Jr.
Merrill, Marie E.
Meyer, Frederick H. and family
Miles, Mildred L.
Miller, Mr. and Mrs. Laymon N.
Miller, Robert E., Jr.
Ming, Mr. and Mrs. Frederick W.
Ming, Roger W.
Morden, Major and Mrs.
   William J.
Morgan, Mrs. Carolyn Good
Moore, Ashley
Moore, Mrs. David Channing
Moore, Lynton G.
Moore, T. Channing, II
Mouzon, Mr. and Mrs.
   James Carlisle
Mouzon, Elizabeth Michel
Mouzon, Margaret Walker

Muller, Frederick W.
Muller, Gertrude
Mumma, Mr. and Mrs. Harries A.
Mumma, Harries A., Jr.
Mumma, James B.
Munro, Eva L.
Neagle, Mrs. Francis E.
Neiley, A. Elizabeth
Neiley, Mr. and Mrs. George F.
Neiley, Virginia Railsback
Neiley, Lt. George Field, Jr.
Nichols, Christine D.
Nichols, Mr. and Mrs. George G.
Nichols, Margaret H. D.
Nobis, Mildred D.
Norvig, John Allen
Norvig, Susan Elizabeth
O'Brien, Mrs. George C.
O'Daniel, Mr. and Mrs. Edgar V.
O'Daniel, Richard Edgar
Oesterheld, Mr. and Mrs.
    Arthur H.
Olewine, Mrs. F. J.
O'Loughlin, Mr. and Mrs.
    Robert R.
O'Loughlin, Jean R.
Oppi, Mrs. Matilda
Oppi, Ethel M.
Oppi, Ruth L.
Packard, Deborah Sands
Packard, Karen Beaumont
Packard, Mrs. Sabra Beaumont
Packard, Sabra Guthrie
Pape, Robert H.
Pape, Walter F.
Pape, Mr. and Mrs. Walter S.
Parker, Mr. and Mrs. Edgar K.
Parton, Charles William
Parton, Mr. and Mrs. George F.
Parton, George F., Jr.

Parton, Sonia
Partridge, Mr. and Mrs. George H.
Peck, Mr. and Mrs. Edward S.
Pedersen, Mrs. Ralph A.
Phillips, Jesse S.
Pinchbeck, Mr. and Mrs. J. A., Jr.
Pinchbeck, Mrs. J. Arthur, Sr.
Pinger, Mr. and Mrs. George C.
Poehl, Ernest
Poehl, Jane K.
Polson, Dr. and Mrs. James A.
Polson, Jean C.
Pontius, Mr. and Mrs. Miller H.
Porter, Edith Underwood
Post, George A.
Powell, John Henderson, Jr.
Powell, Diana Hoyt
Powell, Mrs. Janet Hoyt Rankin
Pullen, Mrs. Richard T.
Purdy, Mrs. A. J.
Quantrell, Mr. and Mrs. Ernest E.
Quantrell, Morton
Quantrell, Virginia
Quinn, Mrs. Maren Lee
Quisenberry, Mr. and Mrs.
    John T.
Ramsey, Mrs. Charlotte C.
Ramsey, Florence L.
Ramsey, James F.
Ramsey, Jane B.
Ramsey, Pauline C.
Redfield, Mrs. Humphrey F.
Reese, Mr. and Mrs. Louis
Reid, Mr. and Mrs. Charles B.
Reynolds, Mr. and Mrs. F. Bradley
Rich, Mr. and Mrs. James P.
Rich, Phebe
Riggs, Mr. and Mrs. Arad
Riggs, Meredith J.
Riggs, Robert M.

Riggs, Dr. and Mrs. William D.
Rinehart, Charles E., Jr.
Roberts, Gwyneth Anne
Roberts, Megan E.
Roberts, Mr. and Mrs. W. Herbert
Robinson, Mr. and Mrs. Leland R.
Robinson, Lucius A.
Robinson, Sarah R.
Roeser, Mr. and Mrs. John E.
Rogers, Dr. and Mrs. Arthur H.
Rogers, John Arthur
Root, Mrs. Donald Scott
Rossiter, Mr. and Mrs. Winton G.
Routh, Mr. and Mrs. E. Edgar
Routh, Nellie B.
Russell, Edith B.
Russell, Mr. and Mrs. Kenneth G.
Russell, Philip W.
Ruston, Mr. and Mrs. Perry L.
Ruston, Robert H.
Rutherford, Mr. and Mrs.
  George P.
Rutherford, Jane M.
Rutherford, Nancy R.
Ryon, Mr. and Mrs. Aymer Mills
Ryon, Inza Manning
Schmid, John H.
Schumann, Mrs. Emma
Seaver, Mr. and Mrs. James T.
Shailer, Mr. and Mrs. William M.
Sherer, Dr. and Mrs. Joseph, Jr.
Simpson, Mrs. James M.
Singmaster, Mr. and Mrs.
  J. Arthur
Singmaster, James A., Jr.
Sitterley, Mr. and Mrs. James E.
Sitterley, Theodore S.
Skinner, Mr. and Mrs. Louis E.
Sloan, Mrs. Jane Quantrell
Smith, Annie Halsey

Smith, Mrs. A. Weston
Smith, Mr. and Mrs. Howard V.
Smith, Howard V., Jr.
Smith, Jennie S.
Smith, Mrs. Joanne Booth
Smith, Mrs. Marion E. Hobbs
Smith, Mary E.
Smith, Mason
Smith, Mr. and Mrs. Philip
Smith, Stephen Herbert
Smith, Susan May
Smith, Mr. and Mrs.
  W. Armstrong
Smyth, Mr. and Mrs.
  William Brice
Smyth, Evelyn Anne
Smythe, Mrs. B. E.
Speer, David S.
Spencer, Mrs. Cynthia Lake
Spencer, Mr. and Mrs. Frank N.
Springer, Marguerite
Stafford, David Frankland
Stafford, Mr. and Mrs.
  Frankland F.
Stafford, Oliver Mead, III
Stauffer, Jack
Stauffer, Patricia
Stauffer, Virginia
Stearns, Katherine
Stearns, Margaret D.
Stearns, Mr. and Mrs. Ralph H.
Steiglitz, Mrs. Annette Campbell
Stenhouse, Mrs. Molly
  Hardenbergh
Stephen, Ina
Stephen, Lily L.
Stephen, Mary Bell
Stetson, Mr. and Mrs. George
Stewart, Mr. and Mrs. Edward N.
Stewart, Edward N., Jr.

Stone, John C.
Stone, Susan R.
Stone, Mr. and Mrs. J. Sydney
Stowell, Carolyn Louise
Stowell, Mr. and Mrs. Kenneth K.
Stowell, Mr. and Mrs. William C.
Stowell, William C., Jr.
Street, O. Dickinson
Swan, Mr. and Mrs. Clinton C.
Swan, Estelle
Swan, Frances S.
Swan, Helen F., Jr.
Sweet, Mr. and Mrs. Charles A.
Sweet, Lt. Charles A., Jr.
Sweet, Lt. Robert R.
Swets, Joan Estelle
Swets, John Edward
Swets, Robert Barker
Sykes, Dr. and Mrs. Lawrence G.
Sykes, Emily
Sykes, Katharine
Syska, Mr. and Mrs. Adolph G.
Syska, Edna
Syska, Robert
Tait, Marguerite I.
Tait, Mrs. W. Ormiston
Taylor, Gardner W.
Tenore, Mr. and Mrs. Louis
Terpening, Mr. and Mrs.
   Herbert S.
Thayer, Morton P.
Thompson, Lorena B.
Thompson, Lorene
Thompson, Marion P.
Thompson, Lt. Col. and Mrs.
   Roger W.
Thompson, Roderic G.
Tier, Mrs. Charles A.
Tilton, Mr. and Mrs. Edgar S.
Tilton, Edgar S., Jr.

Tilton, Florence E.
Tilton, Marie L.
Todd, Mr. and Mrs. Russell W.
Towner, Anna C.
Towner, Mabel E.
Treadwell, Mr. and Mrs.
   John P., Jr.
Treadwell, John P., IV
Trisman, Mrs. Millie K.
Van Duzer, Mr. and Mrs. A. H.
Van Galder, H. C.
Van Gilder, Mr. and Mrs.
   Joseph V.
Van Slyke, Donald D.
Viele, Mrs. Charles L.
Viele, Frances B.
Walker, Mr. and Mrs.
   Harry Leslie
Walker, Harry Leslie, II
Walker, Mr. and Mrs.
   John Blanchard
Walker, Lois Thompson
Walker, Robert C.
Warnke, Lucie M.
Warnshuis, Mr. and Mrs. A. L.
Warren, Harry E. and family
Weaver, Mrs. Frederick
Weaver, Richard L.
Weaver, Ruth L.
Webster, Mr. and Mrs.
   David Frank
Webster, David Kenyon
Webster, John Kingsley O.
Webster, Frank Josiah
Webster, Mr. and Mrs. William H.
Weir, Joseph
Westermann, Mr. and Mrs. H. T.
Weston, Helen K.
Weston, James W.
Weston, Ralph L.

187

Whitlock, Mr. and Mrs. F. B.
Whitten, Mr. and Mrs. Paul
Wilken, Sarah E.
Wilkinson, Esther J.
Willis, Dr. and Mrs. Waring
Wilson, Mr. and Mrs. Douglas H.
Wilson, Dorothy G.
Wilson, Elizabeth T.
Wilson, Mrs. Frank W.
Wilson, Harold T.
Wilson, Harold T., Jr.
Wilson, Helen B.

Wilson, Helena Jane
Wilson, Mr. and Mrs. Leon T.
Wise, Charlotte E.
Woodhull, Lt. and Mrs.
    Daniel E., Jr.
Woodhull, Elizabeth A.
Woodhull, Mr. and Mrs. William T.
Woodhull, William T., Jr.
Worth, Mr. and Mrs. H. C.
Young, Capt. and Mrs. Roger A.
Young, Mary Priestley
Yungel, Mrs. Edward A.

18

COMMITTEE FOR THE CENTENNIAL
NOVEMBER, 1950

Thomas B. Gilchrist, *Chairman*
Howard M. Erskine
Mrs. William Nelson Ferris
Ralph W. Gwinn
Lewis S. Latimer
Mrs. Russell McCandless
Mrs. Neal T. McKee

Harry D. Nims
Mrs. John H. Owen
O. Dickinson Street
Harry Leslie Walker
Mrs. A. L. Warnshuis
Mrs. Franklin S. Whitehouse
Mrs. Francis B. Whitlock

19

THE CHURCH STAFF, 1950-51

Dr. Lowell Russell Ditzen, *Minister*
Dr. Ronald William McNeur, *Assistant Minister*
Mrs. Otto J. Gette, *Director of Religious Education*
Miss Winifred Pietsch, *Director of Nursery School*
Mrs. Helen Powers Revellese, *Executive Secretary*
Mrs. Jean McVicar DuPuy, *Ministers' Secretary*
Mrs. Patricia Doorly Kaufman, *Secretary*
Erich Thieme, *Sexton*
Alan Flewelling, *Assistant Sexton*
Mrs. Elsie Gudos, *Housekeeper*

Note: The former secretary, Miss Marian Brown and the former sexton,
Walter Van Dorn, gave many years of devoted service to the church.

INDEX

189

PRINTED FOR THE CONSISTORY
AT THE PETER PAUPER PRESS
MOUNT VERNON · NEW YORK